Kranti Deep Verma

Emergency and Quest for Total Revolution in India

CANADIAN
Academic Publishing

2015

Emergency and Quest for Total Revolution in India

Kranti Deep Verma

Assistant Professor,
Department of History,
Bhim Rao Ambedkar College,
University of Delhi, Delhi.

CANADIAN
Academic Publishing

2015

Price : $27.86

First Edition : May, 2015

ISBN : 978-1-926488-25-7

ISBN Allotment Agency : Library and Archives Canada (Govt. of Canada)

Published & Printed by
Canadian Academic Publishing
81, Woodlot Crescent,
Etobicoke,
Toronto, Ontario, Canada.
Postal Code- M9W 6T3
Phone- +1 (647) 633 9712
http://www.canadapublish.com

In Loving Memory of Amma, Chacha & Baba

ACKNOWLEDGEMENT

I would like to thank all those who supported me in writing this book. Firstly I pay my gratitude to Dr. R.R. Bakshi, my M.Phil. Research Supervisor who guided me in M.Phil. Research work and boosted my moral. My special thanks to Prof. Ramkuwanre, Dr. G.K. Arora, Dr. S.S. Chawla, Dr. Ravindra Singh, Dr. Arvind Kumar Yadav, Mr. Purushottam & Mr. Sanjay Sharma with whom I exchanged my ideas and interaction with them benifitted me immensely. Library staff of Jawaharlal Nehru University (JNU, New Delhi) & Jamia Millia Islamia, (New Delhi) helped me very much in providing books and sources for doing this work. I am thankful to all of them. My family members consistently supported me during this work. Last but not least my wife Arunim Singh Verma consistently forced me to complete this book despite my laziness.

- Kranti Deep Verma

CONTENTS

INTRODUCTION

In 1970s Indian politics witnessed many changes. A first non- congress government came into power at the centre. Emergency on national level was imposed in the country by Prime Minister Indira Gandhi on the pretext of internal disturbances. Almost all the opposition leaders, persons from Intelligentsia, Academics, press and media were put behind the bars because they opposed the growing concentration of power in few hands. It was the time when veteran leader Jai Prakash Narayan popularly known as 'JP' gave a call for "Total revolution" to youth of this country. Not only youth but people from academics, intelligentsia and press responded warmly and actively to 'Total revolution'.

In a democratic society like India, when a person concentrates more and more power in his/her hands and does not care for the miseries of common man , he is thrown out of the office by the masses, because it is ultimately the public which gives him power (in the from mandate) to rule over them. This right to vote may be said as the "Sharpest weapon in the hands of Public". Elections which held after Emergency showed that the Indian citizen used this weapon effectively.

JP was the man behind this whole political change. He not only inspired and guided the movement but also challenged the Emergency whole heartily though his shattering health was not giving him permission to do so.

JP was not fighting to any individual, but his entire struggle was against that autocratic and corrupt rule which was the greatest blow to democracy in the country. He wanted to bring the change through peaceful means. Impact of Gandhiji's teachings is clearly visible on the thought and working of JP.

Before independence when JP joined the freedom movement, he worked closely with Gandhiji. Even his wife Prabhawati lived at ashram with Gandhiji when JP went to jail in the freedom movement. He became so close to Gandhiji that influence of Gandhism on his personality and working style became undetectable.

JP personally considered Indira Gandhi like her daughter but ideological differences between both the leaders were quite prominent. "Despite many ideological differences between them, JP went to visit Mrs. Gandhi personally at her home. It was his unending love for human being. He blessed her for bright future."[1] While Indira

Gandhi considered nationalization of banks and greater role to public sector against private sector as a means to bring socialism, for JP socialism was meant to give public more and more participation in the power to empower them to participate in democracy at broad scale.

When JP loosened confidence in Marxian Dialectical materialism, he thought it insufficient to bring any change peacefully in the lives of millions of millions human being, he then came near Sarvodaya of Vinoba Bhave. He accepted Vinoba's leadership in Bhudan movement (charity of land). Vinoba observed about JP "There were a politician and a saint in our movement. Jayaprakash was saint and myself politician."[2]

His relationship with socialist leader Ram Manohar Lohia was very intimate and who later on said about him, "He can move the country but the condition is that he himself stands unmoved."[3]

JP wanted radical changes from below to top level in the society. His Total revolution was aimed to bring the changes in the lives of ordinary masses. He believed that we got only political freedom and unless and until we get economic and social freedom, this freedom is meaningless.JP was very eager for social change as he observed "there are rotten customs and manners associated with such things as marriage, birth, death etc. The purging of these evils also falls within the purview of the Total revolution."[4]

Similarly he was critical about the ill effects of the cast system in India. "The cast system among the Hindus is a glaring example of our evil inheritance. From the time of Lord Buddha and may be even from earlier times, attempts have been made to destroy the hierarchical system of cast but it still flourishes in every part of the country. It is time that we blotted out this black spot from the Hindu society and proclaimed and practiced the equality and brotherhood of all men."5

In the words of Dr. Ram Manohar Lohia, ""Caste restricts opportunity. Restricted opportunity constricts ability. Constricted ability further restricts opportunity. Where caste prevails, opportunity and ability are restricted to ever-narrowing circles of the people".6 Dr. Lohia was so serious about the prevailing cast system in India and its harmful effects that he not only focused on its theoretical aspects but he tried to implement his ideas regarding caste system in his political life as well. In his own party, the Samyukta (United) Socialist Party, 'Lohia promoted lower caste candidates both by giving electoral tickets and high party positions. Though he talked about caste incessantly, he was not a casteist -- his aim was to make sure people voted for the Socialist party candidate, no matter what his or her caste. His point was that in order to make the country strong, everyone needed to have a stake in it. To eliminate caste, his aphoristic prescription was, "Roti and Beti", that is, people would have to break caste barriers to eat together (Roti) and be willing to give their girls in marriage to boys from other castes (Beti).'[7]

Total freedom was JP's dream to be materialized by Janta party government, which came into power after Emergency. But it was the greatest irony that whole period of Janta government passed away in fighting among the various factions. It was a coalition government and every party joined the coalition according to their own interests. It was a group of power hungry politicians fighting one another for their vested interests. Though, elections which took place after Emergency thrown out autocratic Indira Gandhi regime but Janta government also could not provide any alternative to it because it also fell due to its internal contradictions.

But the JP movement showed the world that the 'roots of democracy' are deep in India and the society regards democracy as an important instrument to safeguard independence.

Political leaders who emerged from the JP movement became compromising in their later political life. To form the government and to stay in power became the guiding spirit for them. In the era of coalition governments, they not only kept aside the teachings and values of JP but they even formed government with those against whom JP fought all through his life.

Today, many leaders of JP movement are facing charges of corruption and malpractices to win the elections. Politics has become synonym of power and is dominated by criminals and out laws.

In current scenario, this question has become more relevant whether service to people can be a motto in politics or not.JP was an answer to this question not only in the past but in the present as well.

Now a day, politics is dominated by money power and muscle power and it seems impossible for a poor man to contest and win the election.JP had visualized this situation very early. He advocated reforms in the whole election procedure. He felt that the current democratic form which is in practice in our country, where money power and muscle power dominates the politics, can be said only an outer skeleton of democracy, not the real democracy. Ideas and life of JP can provide an important guideline to make this democratic system more humane and more people oriented.

Though, few people think that JP's finest hour came during the time of Emergency but if we scan his whole life chronologically, we find that he was working at grassroots level since very early. During the Quit India Movement, he was involved in it very actively. When the movement was launched, he was behind bars in Hazaribagh. Mahatma Gandhi and other congress leaders were arrested and this news made him restless. "On November 9th, 1942 he along with three other revolutionaries, Yogendra Shukul, Suraj Narayan Singh and Ram Nandan Misra managed to scale the 21 feet high walls of Hazaribagh central jail and escaped."[8]

This news boosted the moral of revolutionaries throughout the country. He was continuously creating problems for colonial rule along with his friends like Ram Manohar Lohia and others. He went underground along with his comrades and formed a small army of freedom fighters known as the Azad Dasta. Some of the top men of the Dasta were Achyut Patwardhan, Mrs. Aruna Asaf Ali and Suraj Narayan Singh. JP was its supreme leader. Arrangements were also made to train young recruits in the jungles of Nepal terai. JP also tried to establish contacts with Azad Hind Fauj of Netaji Subhas Chandra Bose in Burma. British government was very serious about him. It requested the Government of Nepal to cooperate in his arrest and finally 'JP along with his friends were arrested and kept in Hanuman Nagar jail. But before they could be handed over to the Indian police across the border, Azad Dasta led by Suraj Narayan Singh stormed the jail and JP with his friends was rescued.'9 He became a legendary figure in India. As a prisoner he was tortured very much by the British police to extract some unworthy confessions from him but JP did not bend. 'Although all the top leaders of Congress were released by June 1945, JP and Lohia were considered too dangerous for the British government that they were released only in April 1946.'10 His other noteworthy deeds have been mentioned in his biographical chapter- 4 of this work, which shows his immense valor and heroism.

Indira Gandhi's government faced major problems after her tremendous mandate of 1971. The internal structure of the Congress Party had withered following its numerous splits, leaving it entirely dependent on her leadership for its election fortunes. The Green Revolution was transforming the lives of India's vast underclasses, but not with the speed or in the manner promised under Garibi Hatao. Job growth was not strong enough to curb the widespread unemployment that followed the worldwide economic slowdown caused by the OPEC oil shocks.

Gandhi had already been accused of tendencies towards authoritarianism. Using her strong parliamentary majority, she had amended the Constitution and stripped power from the states granted under the federal system. The Central government had twice imposed President's Rule under Article 356 of the Constitution by deeming states ruled by opposition parties as "lawless and chaotic", thus winning administrative control of those states. Elected officials and the administrative services resented the growing influence of Sanjay Gandhi, who had become Gandhi's close political advisor at the expense of men like P. N. Haksar, Gandhi's chosen strategist during her rise to power. Renowned public figures and former freedom-fighters committed to liberty and democracy like Jaya Prakash Narayan, Ram Manohar Lohia and Acharya Jivatram Kripalani now toured the North, speaking actively against her Government.

In June 1975 the High Court of Allahabad found the sitting Prime Minister guilty of employing a government servant in her election campaign and Congress Party work. Technically, this constituted election fraud, and the court thus ordered her to be removed from her seat in Parliament and banned from running in elections for six years.

Gandhi appealed the decision; the opposition parties rallied en masse, calling for her resignation. Strikes by unions and protest rallies paralyzed life in many states. J.P. called upon the police to disobey orders if asked to fire on an unarmed public. Public disenchantment combined with hard economic times and an unresponsive government. A huge rally surrounded the Parliament building and Gandhi's residence in Delhi, demanding her to behave responsibly and resign.

Prime Minister Gandhi advised President Fakhruddin Ali Ahmed to declare a state of emergency, claiming that the strikes and rallies were creating a state of 'internal disturbance'. Ahmed was an old political ally, and in India the President acts upon the advice of an elected Prime Minister alone. Accordingly, a State of Emergency because of internal disorder, under Article 352 of the Constitution, was declared on June 26, 1975.

Even before the Emergency Proclamation was ratified by Parliament, Gandhi called out the police and the army to break up the strikes and protests, ordering the arrest of all opposition leaders that very night. Many of these were men who had first been jailed by the British in the 1930s and 1940s. The power to impose curfews and unlimited powers of detention were granted to police, while all publications were directly censored by the Ministry for Information and Broadcasting. Elections were indefinitely postponed, and non-Congress state governments were dismissed.

The Prime Minister pushed a series of increasingly harsh bills and constitutional amendments through parliament with little discussion or debate. In particular, there was an attempt to amend the Constitution to not only protect a sitting Prime Minister from prosecution, but even to prevent the prosecution of a Prime Minister once he or she had left the post. It was clear that Gandhi was attempting to protect herself from legal prosecution once emergency rule was revoked.

Indira Gandhi further utilized President Fakhruddin Ali Ahmed, to issue ordinances that did not need to be debated in Parliament, allowing her - and Sanjay - to effectively rule by decree. Inder Kumar Gujral, Minister for Information and Broadcasting, resigned to protest Sanjay's interference in his Ministry's work.

The Prime Minister's emergency rule lasted nineteen months. During this time, in spite of the controversy involved, the country made significant economic and industrial progress but at the cost of liberty and democratic rights of its citizens. This was primarily due to the end it put to strikes in factories, colleges, and universities and the repression of trade and student unions. In line with the slogan on billboards everywhere *Baatein kam, kaam zyada*, ("Less talk, more work"), productivity increased and administration was streamlined. Tax evasion was reduced by zealous government officials, although corruption remained. Agricultural and industrial production expanded considerably under Gandhi's 20-point programme; revenues increased, and so did India's financial standing in the international community. Thus much of the urban middle class in particular found it worth their while to contain their dissatisfaction with the state of affairs.

Simultaneously, a draconian campaign to stamp out dissent included the arrest and torture of thousands of political activists; the ruthless clearing of slums around

Delhi's Jama Masjid ordered by Sanjay and carried out by Jagmohan, which left hundreds of thousands of people homeless and thousands killed, and led to the permanent ghettoisation of the nation's capital; and the family planning program which forcibly imposed vasectomy on thousands of fathers and was often poorly administered, nurturing a public anger against family planning that persists into the 21st century.

In 1977, greatly misjudging her own popularity, Gandhi called elections and was roundly defeated by the Janata Party. Janata, led by her longtime rival, Desai and with Narayan as its spiritual guide, claimed the elections were the last chance for India to choose between "democracy and dictatorship." To the surprise of some - mainly Western - observers, she meekly agreed to step down.

Emergency of 1975 came as a severe blow to democracy when almost all the freedoms of citizens were eroded. The Maintenance of Internal Security Act (MISA) was passed by the Indian parliament in 1973 giving the administration and Indian law enforcement agencies immense power like indefinite "preventive" detention of individuals, search and seizure of property without warrants, telephone and wiretapping - in the quelling of civil and political disorder in India, as well as countering foreign-inspired sabotage, terrorism, subterfuge and threats to national security.

Police and administration were used to suppress the political opponent's at large scale. Almost all the opposition leaders were kept behind the bars. Which incidents led towards the imposition of Emergency and what was the JP movement, shall be discussed in second chapter. Memories of Emergency by the prominent figures shall also be included in this chapter.

In the third chapter emergence of Janata party govt. shall be discussed. The nature of coalition governments in India including that of Janata govt. shall also be discussed in this chapter. After Emergency when first non- congress govt. came into power at centre, it marked a big change in contemporary in Indian politics. It broke the dominance of a single party. Public expectations were very high from the Janata govt. as it was thought that the new govt. will be able to bring the radical changes in political and social system to solve the problems of ordinary masses. J.P. gave dreams of socialism and change in his speeches and basically youth were very fascinated and excited about that. But the new govt. failed to provide any radical change and fell down in very short time due to its inner contradictions political rivalries and high political ambitions led towards the decline of Janata Government. It can be said that contemporary leaders of Janata government totally discarded the teachings & values of JP for their own political ambitions.

In the fourth chapter brief biographical information about JP will be given. JP went America for his studies, where he came in contact with Marxian literature & turned a communist. But when he came back and participated in India's freedom movement, his beliefs in communism got decreased because communist in India were opposing 'Quit India Movement' because they were supporting Russia and Britain in their "Peoples war" against Germany. After independence he joined the Sarvodaya movement along with Vinoba Bhave. But later Bhudan movement also could not suffice his quest and desire to bring socio-economic changes in the lives of poor. Later he gave slogan of 'Total Revolution' to bring socialism and create an egalitarian society. Thus, we find constant changes in his ideas. Because JP's thoughts were flexible enough to accommodate new ideas. His ideology was a result of constant thinking and an untiring sprit to serve the people.

Impact of Mahatma Gandhi on JP's thinking was quite prominent, which shaped his ideas and working style. JP had very intimate relationship with GandhiJi. He had deep regard for Mahatma Gandhi though he himself was then a believer in the cult of violence. He said "I bow before the non violence of Mahatma Gandhi, but it is easier for me to fight with a gun."[11] British government arrested him in 1940 on the charge of opposing British war efforts & kept him in Deoli detention camp in Rajasthan, where he smuggled out his famous letter giving detailed instructions to his party men to organize underground revolt against colonial rule. The letter was intercepted and seized by police and his plan was frustrated. The British govt. published the letter in a distorted form and tried to denigrate him in the eyes of the people. At this moment GandhiJi immediately came to his rescue. Mahatma Gandhi dissociating from his violent plans, condemned the British attempt to malign a patriot like JP. He also pleaded to the govt. for the abolition of the Deoli detention camp. The British govt. abolished it and transferred JP to the Hazaribagh central jail in Bihar.

Gandhiji introduced him with Pandit Jawaharlal Nehru and very soon cordial relationship developed between them as JP and Nehru both held radical views. Both leaders were committed to socialism. Nehru invited him to join the Indian National Congress and work for national independence. He also placed JP in charge of the Labour Department of the Congress and posted him at its central headquarters at Allahabad. 'Once, Pandit Nehru had suffered one of the worst indignities of his life at Patna. He could not even address a public meeting at the Wheeler Senate Hall at Patna in face of an angry & hostile audience. But when Pandit Nehru failed, JP, who had accompanied him, succeeded in saving the situation and denouncing the angry demonstrators for their scandalous behavior.'[12]

Restless and struggling hard with the might of a titan against the dark forces of power politics, massive corruption, and demon of communalism, bureaucratic dominance and moral bankruptcy, Jayaprakash Narayan (1902-1979) lived the life of a hero. It was his deep concern for the common man (that earned him the popular prefix "Lok Nayak"), which led him through Marxism and Socialism to Gandhian way.

The change from his own early Marxist phase is reflected in the contrast between his praise for State power in *Why Socialism,* written in 1935 and his censure of it in *From Socialism to Sarvodaya,* more than 20 years later. But, he later went further to find Sarvodaya inadequate in remedying deep-rooted social ills and stressed the need to mobilize mass struggle. He grew increasingly impatient and justified violence if the Government failed to perform, as he announced in New Delhi in 1969.

Born in Bihar, Jaya Prakash Narayan studied in the U.S. when he came in contact with radical socialist ideas. Returning to India in 1929 he worked with the Indian National Congress and formed the Congress Socialist Party in 1934 within the Congress organization.

He took a leading part in the *Quit India Movement (1942-43),* escaping from the high-security Hazaribagh prison. Soon after Independence, he formed a separate political body, the Socialist Party, which was later merged with Kisan Mazdoor Sabha to become Praja Socialist Party.

Following Gandhiji, JP recognized the prime necessity of change in the individual who takes upon himself/herself the task of changing the society. In this lies the whole philosophy of JP's total revolution.

The gist of this concept is presented in his letter to people of Bihar and an extract from the

Notes on Bihar Movement, both written in 1975. Earlier, he had also pleaded for reviving the ancient concept of dharma to suit democracy so as to ensure that the main mould of life remained indigenous. His basic objective is succinctly told in the text reproduced from JP's weekly, *Everyman's*. By 1957, Jayaprakash Narayan had quit active politics and took great interest in Vinoba Bhave's programmes of Bhoodan-Gramdan and soon became known throughout the world as the Sarvodaya leader. In that capacity, JP espoused many a cause as that of Nagaland, of the surrender of dacoits, of Kashmir and communal harmony.

The main quest, however, remained where and what it was, namely a relentless confrontation against corruption, money power and misuse of political authority which seemed to dominate the national scene even after 30 years of parliamentary democracy.

JP could not sit idle when politics began at last to drift to an authoritarian rule. He was imprisoned on the eve of promulgation of Emergency in June 1975 but was released next year on account of shattered health and an unaccountable kidney trouble. But physically weak JP saw in the encircling gloom a ray of hope.

He inspired political parties other than the ruling one to combine as a single Janata Party against dictatorship and the smothering of all freedoms under Emergency regime.

It was his leadership and guidance, which mainly led to the victory of the Janata Party in the March 1977 elections. All went well for a few months.

But unfortunately forces of selfishness, struggle for power and partisanship reasserted themselves and JP was a disillusioned man at the time of his death in October 1979. His long letter to the then Prime Minister, Morarji Desai, reflects his utter disappointment.

In the concluding fifth chapter JP's ideas shall be seen in the context of present problems of corruption and maladministration. Today Indian society face many problems related to everyday life of people, use of money power & muscle power is increasing day by day not only in politics but in every field. There are glaring inequalities with regard to income & wealth in our country. There is huge concentration of wealth in few hands at one side and on the other side farmers are committing suicide because of their inability to pay their debt. It raises the question of our freedom and about our democratic setup. When people are not free from the clutches of hunger, debt and corruption, it forces us to start a new freedom struggle.

But there are rays of hope to bring the change. It seems that change should be started by introducing reforms in election procedure. Thanks to right to information movement which forced the government to pass the Right to Information Act in Indian parliament which empowered the ordinary man to seek information to the responsible authority. People are learning to use "the right to information". It may prove to be an important instrument in the hands of common man in a democratic society like India.

So there are rays of hope to come out from the present dark shell. Thoughts of J.P. can provide a guideline to begin a change.

References

1. Kumar Prashant, *"Meaning of Jai Prakash"*, in Samved, (New Delhi: Samved Foundation, November, 2004), p.121

2. *Ibid.*, p.119

3. Kishan Patnayak, *"JP Andolan ki Etihasikta"*, in Samved, (New Delhi: Samved Foundation, November, 2004), p.110

4. Jaya Prakash Narayan, *"total revolution is necessary"* JP's text of the AIR broadcast of 12 April 1976,(The Great Upheaval some aspects(ed.) S.L.M. Prachand, Abhishek Publication, Chandigarh, 1977)

5. *Ibid.*

6. Niranjan Ramakrishnan's father, K. G. Ramakrishnan was a friend and associate of Dr. Lohia. Niranjan can be reached at njn_2003@yahoo.com. He is working on a website, www.drlohia.com, devoted to the writings and ideas of Rammanohar Lohia, to be released on Lohia's Birth Centenary.

7. *Ibid.*

8. S.K. Ghosh, *"The Crusade and the End of Indira Raj"*, (New Delhi: Intellectual Book Centre, 1978) p.16

9. *Ibid.* p.17

10. *Ibid.*

11. *Ibid.* p.16

12. *Ibid.* pp.17-18

EMERGENCY AND THE JP MOVEMENT

༄꧁ꦏ꧂

On June 26, 1975, Prime Minister Indira Gandhi proclaimed Emergency under Article 352 of Indian Constitution. She did it on the pretext of internal disturbances and promised to return to normally as soon as conditions warranted it. The provisions of fundamental rights and civil liberties under the constitution of India were suspended. Strict censorship was imposed on press by the Govt. of India. Almost every leader of the opposition was kept behind the bars under the Maintenance of Internal Security Act (MISA).

The Maintenance of Internal Security Act (MISA), was a controversial law passed by the India parliament in 1973 giving the Government of Prime Minister Indira Gandhi and Indian law enforcement agencies special powers and authority - indefinite "preventive" detention of individuals, search and seizure of property without warrants, telephone and wiretapping - in the quelling of civil and political disorder in India, as well as countering foreign-inspired sabotage, terrorism, subterfuge and threats to national security.

The legislation gained notoriety for its disregard of legal and constitutional safeguards of civil rights, especially during the period of national emergency (1975-1977) as thousands of innocent people were believed to have been arbitrarily arrested and even tortured, and many hundreds of these people were reported missing.

The legislation was also invoked to validate the arrest of Indira Gandhi's political opponents, including the leaders and activists of the opposition Janata Party.

The 39th Amendment to the Constitution of India placed MISA in the 9th Schedule to the Constitution, thereby making it totally immune from any judicial review; even on the grounds that it contravened the Fundamental Rights which are guaranteed by the Constitution, or violated the Basic structure.

The law was repealed in 1977 following the election of a Janata Party-led government; the 42nd Amendment Act of 1978 similarly removed MISA from the 9th Schedule.

Controversial successors to this legislation include the Terrorism and Disruptive Activities (Prevention) Act and the Prevention of Terrorism

Act, criticized for authorizing excessive powers for the aim of fighting internal and cross-border terrorism and political violence, without safeguards for civil freedoms.

Emergency

"Almost every American of a certain age remembers what he or she was doing on the fateful Friday when the sudden, and shocking, news of President John F. Kennedy's assassination had come in. In this country the same is true about the infamous Emergency with which Indira Gandhi stunned India and the world 25 years ago this day. It was a defining, and infinitely depressing, moment. With a single stroke of the President's pen, the largest democracy on earth was shoved down to the level of tin-pot dictatorships then so ubiquitous in the Third World. Indian democracy was "suspended" though not yet abolished. However, no one knew or could foresee what would follow."[1] writes Inder Malhotra. On the one hand Prime Minister Indira Gandhi was suppressing and destroying freedom of Indians and simultaneously she was hoping to Indians to be calm and cooperate with the government. Inder Malhotra further writes, "Ironically, most Indians first heard of what was afoot well after the heavy lid of repression had been slammed on the country and half an hour before Indira Gandhi took to the radio to announce that the President "has declared a state of Emergency. There is no need to panic". It was a

BBC World Service broadcast at seven- thirty on the morning of June 26 that informed them of large- scale arrests during the night. The most prominent of those taken into custody were Jayaprakash Narayan, better known as J.P., who had become the rallying point of a powerful, nationwide movement for Gandhi's removal from office, and Morarji Desai, her main rival and, at one time, Deputy Prime Minister in her Cabinet."[2]

अडवाना, चरण सिंह गिरफ्तार

THE HINDU

President Proclaims National Emergency

"Security of India Threatened by Internal Disturbances"

Preventive Arrests: Press Censorship Imposed

PM Explains Action

Emergency news covered by a newspaper

REGD. NO. H/SD-23

INDIAN ❀ HERALD

NATIONAL ENGLISH DAILY

Founder & Editor: THAKUR V. HARI PRASAD

SPECIAL SUPPLEMENT

2 Pages   HYDERABAD, Thursday, June 26, 1975   PRICE 15 Paise

EMERGENCY DECLARED
JP, Morarji, Advani, Asoka
Mehta & Vajpayee arrested

Raj Narain, Mody & Chandra Sekhar held

Only hours later J.P., Desai and thousands of their followers were hit by the counter-stroke of the Emergency that Indira Gandhi had planned and honed in rigorous secrecy, with the help of only a few trusted aides, bypassing ministers and bureaucrats concerned, and executed across the country with rare efficiency. Interestingly, opposition leaders were not the only ones to be hauled to jail. So were several prominent figures in Indira Gandhi's own party, such as Mr. Chandra Shekhar, Mr. Krishnan Kant, who later on became Vice-President of India, Mr. Ram Dhan et al. She suspected that they were part of the "conspiracy" led by Jaya Prakash Narayan" against her.

Prime Minister Indira Gandhi along with his second son, Sanjay Gandhi and few of his staunch followers managed the things in a way that news of mass arrest of leaders could not reach in the public next morning. They did so by cutting off electric supply to New Delhi's Fleet Street.

To cling to power and office, Indira Gandhi had to lock up opposition leaders and gag the Press, a large section of which had been attacking her as virulently as J.P. and Desai. At that time there was no electronic media other than the wholly Government-controlled All India Radio and Doordarshan, India's national broadcaster.

The proposition, being heard to this day, that Indira Gandhi was justified in clamping the Emergency but wrong to subject the Press to censorship is absurd. For, an Emergency without Press censorship was not what Indira Gandhi needed or wanted. As Mr. Khushwant Singh has recorded, she had tersely told him, in response to his plea for lifting the curbs on the Press while keeping the Emergency alive: "There can be no Emergency without censorship".

In this context the voice of dispassionate but competent, foreign observers of the Indian scene should also be heeded. For instance, according to Granville Austin, "The imposition of the Emergency was not utterly without justification. Opposition parties' frustration ... had boiled over. The two sides' behavior had combined to stretch democracy until it snapped ... (However), the Emergency's purposes were shown not to be those claimed for it. It was not to preserve democracy but to stop it in its tracks. It was proclaimed to protect the political office of one individual."3

According to Mr. Surendra Mohan, socialist leader and one of J.P.'s confidants, the supreme of the anti-Indira movement was constantly telling leaders of the opposition parties to "unite immediately or you will have to unite in jail". When some of them demurred, J.P. told them that it was Indira Gandhi who had advised the founder-president of Bangladesh, Sheikh Mujibur Rahman, to set up a one-party state in his country (which he had done in February 1975) and she was quite capable of repeating the experiment herself. Evidently, J.P. had lost confidence in Inidra Gandhi's good faith as completely as she had lost in his.

In fact, at a conclave, presided over by J.P. and attended by Mr. Mohan, the idea of starting a "jail bharo (fill the jails") agitation, with a view to forestalling any unexpected move by the Prime Minister, was mooted. It was dropped partly because of the feeling that not many might want to go to prison needlessly and partly because of the complacent belief that Indira Gandhi was at the end of her tether already.

It is all the more remarkable, therefore, that all through those 19 months, she was very particular that everything she did was seen to be within the Constitution. At the same time, she recklessly amended the Constitution itself to suit her purpose of building protective walls around herself and her office. She made the Emergency proclamation and concomitant ordinances immune from judicial review. She amended the Representation of the People Act and two other laws with retrospective effect to ensure that the Supreme Court was left with no option but to overturn the Allahabad verdict. For, the future, she took away from the Supreme Court the authority to adjudicate election disputes relating to the President, the Vice-President, the Prime Minister and the Speaker of the Lok Sabha and transferred it to "a body to be appointed by Parliament". As Nayantara Sahgal commented later, the inclusion of the three other dignitaries was akin to "light musical accompaniment to the somber theme of Prime Minister Power".

Mercifully, a profoundly more shocking amendment, though approved by the Rajya Sabha as soon as it was placed before it on August 9, 1975, was allowed to lapse. Had it been enacted, anyone holding the offices of President, Prime Minister and Governor of a State would have been granted total immunity from criminal and civil proceedings for any act committed in official or personal capacity, whether before assuming the relevant office or while holding it! Quite clearly, the decision to quietly drop this measure, the Fortieth Amendment, could have been taken by Indira Gandhi alone. But there is evidence to show that she was influenced by the argument of Mr. C.

Subramaniam and some others that the public might think she had "some skeletons in her cupboard". She was also conscious that foreign reaction to this measure would be extremely negative.[4]

Background of JP Movement

This happened not because of any single incident or any single reason but the circumstances were growing since 1973. By the beginning of 1973 Indira Gandhi's popularity began to decline. People's expectations were unfulfilled. Very little was done to overcome the rural and urban poverty and economic inequality. Caste and class oppression was growing in rural areas.

Inder Malhotra observed the situation "For, the J.P. movement, as it was called, had apparently gained great momentum in preceding months. This was so, partly because of the Prime Minister's style of governance, especially her intolerance of any dissent, and partly because of massive economic discontent, caused by drought, inflation and mismanagement on the one hand and by a four-fold increase in world oil prices on the other. Above all, the political and moral authority of Mrs. Gandhi, at its peak after the liberation of Bangladesh, had slumped precipitately. Principally because of the burgeoning corruption and abuse of authority by her acolytes in a party that had turned into an "inverted pyramid" - totally dependent on her, undisturbed by the complete absence of inner-party democracy and happy to wallow in crass, competitive sycophancy of 'The Leader'.5 The verdict of Allahabad high court regarding election of Prime Minister of Mrs. Indira Gandhi for Lok Sabha played a prominent role in deteriorating the situation further and the opposition parties viewed that at this moment Indira Gandhi had no moral right to stay in the office. Inder Malhotra rightly observed "After the Allahabad High Court's judgment on June 12, accompanied by the Congress party's defeat in the Gujarat Assembly elections (which a reluctant Indira Gandhi had held only because of a protest fast by Desai), her delirious critics were convinced that her legal authority, too, had collapsed. For the court had convicted her of "corrupt electoral practices" and debarred her from elective office for six years. J.P. and his gleeful colleagues were confident that she had no option but to resign. When she gave no indication of doing so, they stepped up their ongoing agitation against her steeply."6

On June 24, the Supreme Court, going by established precedents, gave the Prime Minister only conditional stay of the Allahabad verdict, not the unconditional one she had sought. J.P., and his countless followers now became in a very active mood and JP himself became restless for his undying commitment for liberty & democracy. Next day in a massive rally in New Delhi's Ramlila Grounds, "he announced a plan of daily demonstrations in not merely Delhi but also every State capital and district headquarters until Indira Gandhi threw in the towel." He then renewed his appeal to the Army, the police and the bureaucracy "to refuse to obey Indira" and "abide by the Constitution instead".[7] Morarji Desai went much further and told the Italian journalist, Ms. Oriana Fallaci: "we intend to overthrow her to force her to resign. For good ... Thousands of us will surround her house and prevent her from going out...day and night."[8]

Despite all these demands and moral pressure she was not ready to leave the office. For her part, Indira Gandhi was not ready to give up power even for a few days, leave alone a few months needed by the Supreme Court to pronounce on her appeal. All those anxious to preserve their own perches in the power-structure resting solely on the pillar of Indira Gandhi's personality, begged of her not to leave even momentarily, arguing that this was precisely what her and the country's "enemies" wanted. Above all, Sanjay Gandhi, by now the second most powerful person in India, ordained that the "nonsensical" idea of temporary withdrawal must not even be mentioned.

Economic Condition

Economic situation was deteriorating day by day and growing unemployment, rampant inflation and scarcity of foodstuffs created a serious crisis. At this particular time there were nearly 10 million Bangladeshi refugees in India. It was a big burden on Indian economy. The burden of feeding and providing shelter to these refugees had depleted the grain reserves of India. Bangladesh war of 1971 forced the Government of India for a large budgetary deficit. During war anywhere in the world all the resources go towards the war front to fulfill the needs of military. India had to pay a large amount of money to ensure the defeat of Pakistan army. As a result foreign exchange reserves of country were drained out. The drained foreign reserves further increased the budgetary deficit and deepened the economic crisis.

Monsoon rain failed for two years in succession during 1972 and 1973 which led towards terrible drought in most parts of India. As a result there was a massive shortage of food grains and ultimately rises in their prices.

"The drought led to decreased power generation and combined with the fall in agricultural production, and therefore in the demand for manufactured goods, led to industrial recession and rise in unemployment. Same year, the Indian economy witnessed the notorious oil-shock when world prices of crude oil increased four- fold, leading to massive increase in the prices of petroleum products and fertilizers. Prices rose continuously by 22% in 1972-73 alone."[9]observed Bipan Chandra. There was scarcity of essential consumer goods due to price rise which affected both poor and middle classes. Food riots were reported in several parts of the country. These all economic problems created great anger among citizens which came out in the form of protests and processions. Economic problems led to large scale industrial unrest and a wave of strikes in different parts of the country during 1972 and 1973, culminating in all India railway strike in may 1974 which lasted for 22 days. At the end the strike was broken and labour class lost confidence in the leadership of Mrs. Indira Gandhi.

Situation of Law and Order

The situation of Law and order in the country deteriorated particularly during 1974-75.Strikes, student movements and agitations sometimes turned violent. Many universities and colleges were closed sine die indiscipline and violence. In May 1973, there was a mutiny in U.P. by Provincial Armed Constabulary (P.A.C.) which clashed with the army sent to discipline it, which resulted in the death of 35 constables and soldiers.

An efficient and firm leadership was required to tackle the deteriorating law and order situation and that was completely missing. The political scenario was getting worse because cases of corruption were coming to light everyday and degrading morality amongst the leaders had become the order of the day. Congress party as an organization was proving inefficient and incapable of dealing with the political problems at the grassroots level. Corruption was dominating in every walks of life and it was a common belief amongst the masses that people sitting on the higher level of ruling Congress party and government were involved in corrupt malpractices and nepotism. Even Prime Minister Indira Gandhi's son Sanjay Gandhi was using his power to influence the official decisions to benefit his near and dear ones. He was given a license to manufacture 50000 Maruti cars every year despite much criticism. He was not having any kind of experience of operating such manufacturing units. His only qualification was that he was son of a sitting Prime Minister.

Increasing Corruption

Corruption was noticeable in every walk of life very clearly and it was understood by many that many senior congress party leaders are involved in unethical malpractices from top to bottom. It was alleged that Prime Minister Indira Gandhi gave a license to manufacture 50000 Maruti cars to her inexperienced son Sanjay Gandhi. Union cabinet led by Prime Minister India Gandhi proposed the production of a 'People's car' – cheap and affordable with efficient indigenous machine that middle class citizens could afford. Sanjay Gandhi having no experience and understanding of operating such business, completely unaware about the methodology of any design proposal or tie-ups with any firm was awarded exclusive manufacturing license. Prime Minister Indira Gandhi was criticized hugely for promoting this kind of clear favoritism in public life. It is another thing that the car manufacturing unit "Maruti Udyog" founded by Sanjay Gandhi did not produce even a single vehicle during his lifetime. But later on it developed into a India's premier car manufacturing company. But Bangladesh Liberation War and decisive victory over Pakistan made Indira Gandhi so popular in the masses that this issue was drowned. Congress party won elections with huge margins and thus Indira Gandhi became more powerful in Indian politics.

During Nehru's PrimeMinistership it was largely the administration which was corrupt but with the emergence of Indira Gandhi's leadership, corruption of political institutions had become inescapable with the rise of the corrupt politicians and their pathological obsession with personal power. The Times of India wrote "The corruption had assumed many sided character. It had not only made the electoral process a big force, but had helped the emergence of class of corrupt politicians who had captured seats of power at all levels. It had virtually become impossible for an honest congressman to survive within the congress organization".[10]

Further their major social groups got detached from congress party, the middle classes because of price rise and corruption, the rich peasantry, because of the threat land reform and the capitalist, because of the talk of socialism, nationalization of banks and coal mining and antimonopoly measures.

Student Agitations

Educational institutions can be said as the knowledge houses of our society. No society can prosper without generating new ideas and innovations to meet the challenges of the day simultaneously Universities, colleges and schools are the fields where our next generation is prepared. Our future depends on the kind and quality of education and values we cultivate in our youngsters. If these institutions are not in good condition then better future of our youngsters and our society cannot be ensured. The complete educational structure of country at this particular juncture of time was rotting and marred with corruption and mismanagement. The students were agitating for educational reforms and educational opportunities. There was a virtual chaos on the campuses of major universities in Gujarat, Bihar, U.P. and West Bengal. The vice- chancellors and teachers were gheraod daily and the university examinations had become a big farce because of large scale copying by the students had no faith in the educational system because the current system was not guaranteeing to secure jobs after the completion of educational courses.

Labour Movements

Due to ever increasing prices of essential consumer goods, the organized workers were in the streets demanding wage increases. Organized workers were basically in the big cities and political parties knew their strength very well. Political parties were running after the workers because the trade union movement in the country, especially from late 1960s onwards, had virtually become independent of political control. Due to rising prices neither socialism nor communism but economy had become a guiding principle of the working class movement in the country. Indira Gandhi government in spite of taking note of these problems started suppressing the demands and agitations forcefully.

"India Gandhi and her Government had ample means in their legal armory to deal with it. This was underscored by the ruthlessness with which she crushed the railway strike masterminded by Mr. George Fernandez with the avowed objective of "paralyzing" and "starving" the country."[11] Writes Inder Malhotra.

Political Stagnation

There were more than thirty political parties in the country which were registered with in the Election Commission. The opposition parties had lost all hopes of capturing political power through elections. They had only strategy of alliance and fronts to form the Government. They miserably failed to win the hearts of masses and provide a stable government that could fulfill the public's aspirations.

Due to ruling party's policies the public was getting detached increasingly. The middle classes were unhappy due to inflation and corruption. They were forced to pay heavily for essential goods of daily life. No one could dream of getting his work done in a government office without giving bribe.

Government was continuously talking about implementation of land reforms, it was threatening to the rich peasants. The capitalist were unhappy with the government's radical initiatives taken in the field of business and banking sectors. Many banks and natural resources like coal mines were nationalized so capitalists were disenchanted with the ruling government. Apart from all such measures the anti monopoly initiatives adopted by the government in the field of manufacturing and business further turned capitalist away from the government and Congress party.

The opposition party's lost faith in political system in desperation and to remove Congress Party from the power became their single point agenda. The opposition parties were not in a position to defeat Congress separately or collectively as they were defeated badly by the Congress party in the elections of 1971. They were not willing to wait till next general elections but were eager to blindly support any movement which could dethrone the ruling Congress party.

The self- centered politicians were controlling the political system and the political parties became helpless spectators of Aaya Rams and Gaya Rams who were daily changing their loyalties to serve their self – interests. Politics had become devoid of moral principles and urgently needed a pressure of the people's power. J.A. Naik observed the situation, "With the emergence of the rural rich in our state legislatures personal power rather than social idealism became the principle motivation of a politician".[12]

Gujarat Movement

At a time when Congress party was losing popular support and opposition parties had become helpless, the students in Gujarat launched (Jan, 1974) a struggle against the corrupt Congress Government in the state under the auspices of their own organization known as Nava Nirman Yuva Samiti and demanded for the resignation of the Chiman Bhai Patel ministry. Popular anger was due to rise in the prices of food grains, cooking oil and other essential goods. The movement aroused in the form of a student movement and later on joined by the opposition parties. According to Bipan Chandra, "For more than ten weeks the state faced virtual anarchy with strikes, looting, rioting and arson, and efforts to force M.L.A.s to resign."[13]

The Police and government machinery was used on large scale to crush the movement which relied mostly on excessive force, indiscriminate arrests and frequent recourse to lathi-charge and firing.

But the movement was successful in mobilizing people against the state government because it was directly related to the everyday life of common man. Power of people's struggle in a democratic society once again showed and proved its prominence in democracy. The opposition parties had merely supported the agitation; it was led by the students themselves. As one opposition MP said in the Lok Sabha debate: the boys had succeeded where men had failed and the students had succeeded where the politicians had failed." Under huge pressure, the central government, by February, was forced to ask the state government to resign, suspend the assembly and impose President Rule in the state. Continued agitation and a fast unto death by Morarji Desai forced Prime Minister Indira Gandhi in March 1975 to dissolve the assembly and announce fresh elections to it in June.

The Gujarat movement was the great moral booster not only to the students but to the opposition parties also. It can be said that a social movement gave birth to a political movement.

Bihar Movement

In 1974, JP devoted himself to the peasants' struggle. He founded, together with V. M. Tarkunde, the "Citizens for democracy" in 1974 and the "People's Union for Civil Liberties" in 1976, NGOs to uphold and defend civil liberties. In Bihar students were agitating similarly as in Gujarat. JP took over leadership of student's movement in Bihar and demanded resignation of the congress government and dissolution of assembly. 'He gave a call for "Total revolution" (5 June 1974) or "a struggle against the very system which has compelled almost everybody to go corrupt".[14]

He asked the students and the people to put pressure on the existing legislators to resign, paralyze the government, gherao the state assembly and government offices, setup parallel people's government all over the state, and pay no taxes.

'He led a silent procession at Patna on April 8, 1974. Next day students conferred title of "Loknayak" on him. He supported the demand of dissolution of assembly after the firing case of Gaya district which took place on April 12, 1974. Further on June 5, 1974, he gave an application to the Governor of Bihar containing many lakhs signatures and in a huge rally gave a call for "Total Revolution" in August, 1974. Speaking in a General meeting at Patna he called to bring moral revolution by eradicating corruption from our public life. On October-3, 4, 5, 1994 total Bihar was closed down.[15]

JP Movement

JP decided to go beyond Bihar and organize a country- wide movement against widespread corruption and for the removal of congress and Indira Gandhi, who was now seen as a threat to democracy and as a fountainhead of corruption.

JP's total revolution had a wider appeal to the different sections of the society. Its course was to remove the government. As he said, he was not "interested in this or that ministry being replaced or the Assembly being dissolved". His fight was for the over haul of the socio- economic system and "for a real people's democracy."[16]

Multi- Dimensional Thrust

The youth was the core of JP's strength. The movement was said to solve the problems of unemployment and to reform the educational system. The character of demands that Sri Jaya Prakash Narayan had presented to parliament on March 6, 1975 on behalf of the people of India is specific regarding the objectives of the revolution. Concerning educational reforms it says:-

1. Education must be the instrument of the creation of a society based on the ideals enshrined in this character, and should lead to modernization instead of westernization.
2. Effective steps must be taken to raise the quality and content of education in keeping with national requirements. The present pattern must be revised at every level.
3. Vocationalasation of education from the secondary stage coupled with a system of economic planning guaranteeing employment. A university degree should not be a requirement for any but academic jobs.
4. Higher priority to achieving universal primary education and universal adult education within five years.
5. Check on government interference in the educational institutions. The management of these instructions should ordinarily be entrusted to their respective teaching staff along with democratic student participation.

Crusade against Corruption

Corruption was a problem of great concern for JP "Corruption is eating into the vitals of our political life"[17] said the charter of demands. One of the great failures of the form of democracy in our country is its inability to check corruption of political institution and not necessarily that of individuals. There are ways to punish a corrupt politician but there is a less chance to compel the political parties to collect and spend money in permissible limits under public security. The election system had become hopelessly corrupt. Although there was a check on the election expenses incurred by the candidate, there was no such provision for political parties.

When the opposition had no jeeps, ruling congress had the planes and such an utterly unequal fight was going on in the name of democracy and free elections. JP wanted to check it. In an open letter addressed to the youth for democracy in December 1973, he said "the most serious danger comes from violation of the democratic process since independence; elections have been growing more and more irreverent to the people and to the democratic process".

"The reason is that money, falsehood, corruption and physical force have combined together to erode steadily the very meaning and substance of elections."[18]

"The corruption had assumed many- sided character. It had not only made the electoral process a big farce, but had helped the emergence of a class of corrupt politicians who had captured seats of power at all levels. It had virtually become impossible for an honest congressman to survive within the congress organization. The character of demands that JP had presented to the speaker of Lok Sabha, i.e. upper house of parliament of India was specific on this score and demanded some concrete steps to remove corruption from public life. He had demanded appointment of high powered judicial tribunals to investigate into allegations of corruptions against persons in high positions, including the prime minister and chief ministers and implementation of the recommendations of Santhanam committee. It wanted the holders of public office to declare their assets periodically."[19]

The Charter of demands made specific proposals for holding free and fair elections. It proposed for the implementation of the unanimous recommendations of the Joint Parliamentary Committee on electoral reforms, the inclusion of election expenses incurred by the political parties into the election expenses of the candidates, constitution of multi member election commission, counting of the votes at the polling booths, ban on the movement of private vehicles on the election day and enforcement of prohibition on that day etc.

Times of India wrote, "When the political institutions get corrupted by corrupt and power-drunk politicians the rule becomes oppressive, authoritarian and dictatorial. The proclamation of

Emergency was an inescapable culmination of the rule that had relied upon repressive measures than reforms to prolong its course. The JP movement was addressed to the restoration of democratic rights and civil liberties to the people. It had demanded immediate withdrawal of the Emergency which was in force since 1971, the repeal of MISA and DIR, granting of full political and the trade union rights to teachers, students and the workers in industrial and commercial establishment."[20]

JP movement focused on a point to bring about decentralization of political power in the society and create genuinely self governing institutions right from the village level onwards. It is essential that people keep a check on the holders of political power if the political system is to check corruption of power.

Another thrust of the JP movement was the creation of a national alternative to the ruling party.JP was conscious of his responsibility for creating unification of the non-communist opposition forces in the country and did strive towards this end. The emergence of Janata party was the culmination of such efforts by JP and others.JP and his movement for total revolution provided a platform for the Jana Sangh, Congress (o), BLD and the socialist party to come together. He worked tirelessly and advocated for the necessity of creating a national alternative to the ruling party.

Organizational Structure

JP movement required its own organizational structure for the realization of its objectives. Much of India's political strength lay outside the fold of the opposition parties, this was more so when JP movement was launched.

At the apex there was a National Jan Sangharsh Samiti, which was composed of the representatives of the National opposition parties who were supporting the movement. JP decided not to take any post but to guide the movement from above. Then there were provincial and district level Jan Sangharsh Samitis. Since the students formed the core of the movement's strength, there was a special organization for them-"Chatra Yuva Sangharsh Vahini. He considered Vahini as the vehicle of the revolution. Chatra Yuva Sangharsh Vahini with a view to building up a trained cadre of young workers for the cause of Total Revolution. Elaborating the programme of work which he thought for the Sangharsh Vahini, he said in an interview in 1977, "I expect them to work in close cooperation with the village and ward sabhas or people 'committees, consisting of all citizen of the area, and to function as their vanguard. In fighting against all the types of injustice and oppression. In particular, they have to engage themselves in organizing the harijans and other weaker sections of society. Apart from this they are expected to work or the acceleration of the social change and the introduction of necessary structural reforms in the economic life of the people of the area. If and when a situation develops calling for a local, regional or national struggle either by way of protest against injustice and oppression or for ushering in a new social order, they are expected to play a leading role in it. I must make it clear that I do not see any protest for total revolution without a long drawn out struggle and with the masses participating in such a struggle."[21]

At the subsequent stages of the movement, the Janata governments were formed at the village level in many Bihar villages. The Janata government was to collect taxes from people and provide its own parallel administration. The members of these Janata governments were elected directly by the people.

JP hoped that if these two organizations took roots, a powerful nucleus would be built up, which would not merely ensure that genuine representatives of the people got elected in the next elections, but would also carry forward the work of Total Revolution in various walks of life. He wrote, "I might say that if my life is spared for a few years, it might be possible for me to compel the new rulers of Bihar to come out of their comfortable homes and offices to face the reality of poverty stricken and backward Bihar. That could be done only if the students and people's struggle committees were to continue to function and exercise enough influence over their representatives, not only to make them carry out their promises but also to participate actively in the people's continuing revolutionary struggle."[22]

In March 1974, JP led a huge procession at Delhi and presented a Charted of Demands to the speaker of Lok Sabha on behalf of public.

JP repeatedly toured the whole country and mobilized masses especially in Delhi and other parts of north India. Prime Minister Mrs. Indira Gandhi challenged JP movement to test its popularity in the coming General elections, due in February-March 1976.JP accepted the challenge and his supporting parties decided to form a National coordination committee.

Now it appeared that the issue will be solved very soon trough electoral means. But a sudden twist to Indian politics was given by a judgment on 12th June 1975 by justice Sinha of Allahabad High Court, on an election petition by Raj Narayan, convincing Mrs. Indira Gandhi for having indulged in corrupt campaign practices and declaring her election invalid. The judgment also meant that she could not seek election to parliament or hold office for six years and therefore continue as Prime Minister.

Prime Minister Mrs. Indira Gandhi refused to step down from the office and appealed to Supreme Court. While the Supreme Court would hear her appeal on 14 July, justice V.R. Khrisna Iyer, the vacation judge of the supreme court, created further confusion when he decided on 24 June that, till the final disposal of her appeal by the full bench of the supreme court, Mrs. Gandhi could stay in office and speak in parliament but could not vote in it.

Gujarat assembly elections results came on 13 June. The opposition Janata front won 87 seats and congress 75 seats in a house of 182.

The Allahabad high court judgment and Gujarat assembly elections gave a boost to JP movement. The opposition parties accused Mrs. Gandhi of 'clinging to an office corruptly gained' demanded her resignation and called for country-wide campaign to for the issue.

The climax of JP movement came on 25 June 1975 when a public call was given by JP for a nation-wide mass civil disobedience movement. It was said that people will start Satyagrah at the prime minister's residence from the next day for a period of seven days only. Then it has to be shifted in other provinces. The Satyagrah was planned to be conducted only till Supreme Court verdict in Indira Gandhi's disqualification case was not coming. Here the role of Morarji Desai seems quite suspicious in a sense that he modified the programme of satyagrah which was to be started on 26th June 1975. JP in his letter to Prime Minister Mrs. Indira Gandhi which he wrote on 21st July 1975 from Chandigarh prison clearly said that there was no such plan to paralyze the government and if there was any plan like this, it was for a short while. The essence of declared plan was that Prime Minister should resign until her Supreme Court verdict was not coming. In support of this demand few people were about to start satyagrah only for few days. The programme was to be conducted for seven days in New Delhi after that in other provinces and this was to be done only till the verdict of supreme court. There was no plan of coup d'état. But Morarji Desai on the evening of 25th June 1975 gave an interview; he said "we intend to overthrow her, to force her to resign. For good.... Thousands of us will surround her house to prevent her from going out or receive visitors. We'll camp there night and day shouting to her resign."23

Thus evidences shows that leaders around JP were not totally integrated with his plans and spirit of satyagrah. It seems that Morarji was going on his own way and he saw a great opportunity in the JP movement to serve his vested interest.

Emergency blow

Under these threats Prime Minister Mrs. Indira Gandhi proclaimed a state of Internal Emergency under Article 352 of the Indian Constitution on the morning of June 26, 1975, suspending the normal political process. Although an Emergency was already in the force since the preceding four year and the opposition parties were demanding its revocation. All the opposition parties observed April 6th as the 'lift- emergency day' all over India, held meetings and demanded the revocation of Emergency.

The proclamation of an "Internal Emergency" suspended the fundamental rights and civil liberties. Strict censorship was imposed on the press. Almost all the main opposition leaders were arrested in early hours of 26th June under the Maintenance of Internal Security Act (MISA). Among those leaders were Jai Prakash Narayan, Morarji Desai, Atal Bihari Vajpayee and congress dissidents such as Chandra Shekhar. Several academics, newspersons, trade union leaders were put behind the bars. Arrests continued throughout the period of Emergency and it is estimated that in all, more than 100000 were arrested during a period of 19 months.

During the emergency period the parliament was made ineffective. The opposition of a few brave MPs, who had not been arrested, was nullified as their speeches were not permitted to report in the press.

There was direct control on the state governments. The two non-congress governments, DMK in Tamil Nadu and Janata in Gujarat were dismissed in January and March1976 despite being quite complaint. The congress chief ministers of U.P. and Orissa were replaced for not being reliable enough. The congress party itself was controlled strictly. There was no internal democracy within the congress party.

A series of decrees, laws and constitutional amendments reduced the powers of the judiciary. The defense of India act and the MISA were amended in July 1975 to the determent of the citizen's liberties. In November 1976, an effort was made to change the basic civil libertarian structure of the constitution through its 42nd Amendments. It was laid down that there would be no limitation whatever on the power of parliament to amend the constitution. Fundamental rights were indirectly emasculated by being subordinate to an expanded version of the Directive Principles of state policy embedded in the Constitution of India. The intelligentsia, teachers, journalists, professionals, small town lawyers and middle classes in particular viewed the 42nd amendment to the Constitution, passed in September 1976 as an effort to subvert democracy by changing the very basic structure of the Constitution.

To divert attention from the monstrosity that she had perpetrated, Indira Gandhi made the most of her Twenty-Point Programme, to which Sanjay added his five points, and never stopped talking of how the Emergency would become an engine of social justice and change, indeed a boon for the poor. At the end of the day nothing much happened, however. On the contrary, the credibility of her programme and her own took a sharp knock because of her constantly shifting positions and claims.

For example, she at first advertised the existence of non- Congress (I) Governments in Tamil Nadu and Gujarat as proof that the Emergency did not mean her dictatorship, only an attempt to "put back on the track" the Indian democracy that had got "derailed". Within months she declared that these States were the "two islands of indiscipline" that needed to be sorted out. She imposed President's rule in Tamil Nadu and brought down the Janata Front ministry in Ahmadabad by the time-honored technique of effecting defections from it.

A very significant development which took place during Emergency was emergence of Sanjay Gandhi, younger son of Prime Minister Mrs. Indira Gandhi, who held no office in the government but became an extra-constitutional centre of power. By April 1976 Sanjay Gandhi emerged as a parallel authority, interfering at will in the working of the government and administration. He was courted and obeyed by cabinet ministers and senior civil servants. From the second half of 1976 the youth congress led by Sanjay Gandhi became more important than the parent organization.

Sanjay Gandhi put forward his 4 points which gradually became more important than the official twenty points.

The points were-

- Don't take dowry at the time of marriage.
- Practice family planning and limit families to only two children.
- Plant trees.
- Promote literacy.

He was also determined to beautify the cities by clearing slums and unauthorized structures impending roads, bazaars, parks, monuments etc.

The government was incited by Sanjay Gandhi,

decided to promote family planning more vigorously and even in an arbitrary, illegitimate and authoritarian manner. Incentives and persuasion were increasingly replaced by compulsive and coercive methods and above all by compulsory sterilization. Government servants, school teachers, and health workers were assigned arbitrarily fixed quotas of number of persons they had to motivate to undergo sterilization. The police and administration used repressive and forceful measures to the enforcement of the quotas. The most affected were rural and urban poor who often protested in all sorts of everyday may, including recourse to flight, hiding and rioting.

In the extremely hostile political environment, Sanjay Gandhi, the second son of Prime Minister Indira Gandhi rose to prominence and most near and dear advisor of her. Sanjay Gandhi's influence increased over government dramatically, though he was neither an official in the government nor an elected political leader. His only eligibility was being the son of Prime Minister which became the most important and deciding factor in his increased role in the government. Sanjay started influencing many cabinet ministers and high ranking government officials in day to day working. While many of them bowed down before the autocratic son of Prime Minister, few men protested and resigned. New men were appointed on the posts of these protesting officials and in this way the tyrannical methods of Sanjay got legitimating. Inder Kumar Gujral who later on became Prime Minister of India, resigned from the

Ministry of Information and Broadcasting when Sanjay Gandhi tried to interfere in the internal affairs of his ministry. He ignored to obey the directions of an unelected person in a democratic setup and opted to quite.

Sanjay Gandhi launched a drive to make Delhi free from the slum areas. Slum dwellers were forced to leave the city. Sanjay reportedly instructed the officials of Delhi Development Authority which was headed by his close associate Jagmohan, to rinse the heavily populated area near Turkman Gate and Jama Masjid. About 10000 grungy huts were destroyed and around 800 people died in this cleansing drive operated under the guidance of Sanjay Gandhi.

Another step initiated by Sanjay Gandhi which acclaimed much criticism was widespread family planning program implemented brutally and forcefully. His vision for India was a contained population growth and a nation free of crowding. It was believed that administrative and police officials have been assigned quotas to perform vasectomies among the men. Administrative machinery used brute force to meet the targets and in some cases women were also sterilized forcefully. Though, it was officially stated that men having two or more children had to go through vasectomy voluntarily, but it is believed that several unmarried young men, political opponents and poor were forcefully sterilized. The horrifying memories of this family planning drive still haunts many Indians and is being criticized publically for creating a public aversion to family planning which had a lasting impact on the Government Progammes for the forthcoming years. After that family planning programmes have been always secondary priorities for the political parties and governments.

Similar methods were applied in anti encroachment drive to beautify the capital. Several structures were forcefully demolished by administrative machinery which further increased the existing climate of fear and repression.

Repressive Measures

According to Inder Malhotra, "Over 100000 were jailed without trial. This was twice the number of arrests during the 1942 Quit India movement throughout the subcontinent. Twenty custodial deaths took place; a Kerala detainee, Rajan, disappeared without a trace. In the name of beautification of cities and towns, poor people were uprooted from their dwellings. A fear psychosis took over the country. Since authoritarianism breeds arrogance, those clothed in temporary authority settled many a personal score. Corruption increased by leaps and bounds. It was the terror unleashed by vasectomies that became Indira Gandhi's Nemesis and contributed the most to her humiliating defeat in the 1977 elections."[25]

Many contemporary newsmen and literary figures who faced the atrocities of emergency view Emergency rule as one of the darkest chapters of Indian history and nothing that happened during the British rule is comparable to large-scale sterilization of the poorest and the helpless, their sufferings and the tortures of political prisoners. Total eradication of the congress party in the northern Indian in the Election held after emergency showed the people rebellion against the forcible sterilization measures. It was reported by many newspapers that many of the villagers in some northern states were not sleeping in their villages for months for fear of being carried to the sterilization camps. They were sleeping in their fields. Around a dozen places police was reported to disperse the crowd. Times of India reported "Many people lost their lives in a pitched six hour battle with armed police in both the town of Muzaffarnagar and surrounding countryside."[26]

There was nothing wild or exaggerated, however, about what the bush telegraph said concerning the police firing at Delhi's Turkman Gate where slums were demolished and those living in them "relocated". Soon thereafter, gunfire was heard also at Muzaffarnagar, a town in Uttar Pradesh, 100 km away from the national capital. Above all, forced vasectomies, in pursuance of one of the five points in Sanjay's personal agenda, were to spread both fear and revulsion across North India. I will return to this subject presently but first it is necessary to review what Indira Gandhi tried to do with the Emergency and how the various institutions of the Indian State behaved during those troubled and agonizing times.

Jasbir Singh, a student of Jawaharlal Nehru University, was arrested and he told his own story: "A sub-inspector by name Tekchand took me into the police custody. Some policemen were called in. They started beating me with chappals and shoes from all sides. This went on from six in the evening to late at night. The following day they tied my hands and feet to two chairs and started swinging me. I vomited blood. They threatened to kill me, if I revealed the beating to anybody. On 25th June, late at night, I was taken to sub-inspector Tekchand. He placed a 7 feet long and 8 inch thick heavy wood on my neck; my hands were tied down to it from behind and I was hanged in that state for about an hour. I lost my consciousness; started vomiting the blood again. The following day the same torture was repeated. I was mercilessly beaten; they pulled my hairs and thus removed them. My face and head was full of blood and wounds. I was not given any medical treatment."[27]

Sadhana further reported, "Bhanusudan Bhate, a high school teacher from Nagothe in the Kolaba district of Maharashtra, was arrested on 24th December 1975. He was mercilessly beaten from all sides by eight persons at a time. They threw him on a wall. The next day he was forced to lie down. They put a big wooden rod on his leg and started dancing on it. The following days, when he was carrying high fever, he was again beaten. His eardrums were broken. All this was done to exact some information about one Mr. Dixit, which he never had.[28]

According to Inder Malhotra "With all due respect, it must also be recorded that the highest Judiciary, too, disappointed the country. Some High Courts showed courage, most notably in releasing detenus, despite the suspension of fundamental rights including the right of habeas corpus. But when all the habeas corpus cases were bunched together and transferred to a five-member bench of the Supreme Court, things changed."[29]

The police used brutal method to torture the satygrahis. Many political persons died in the prison or were kept there until they reached the stage. JP himself was released when he became clear to the authorities that he would not survive more than few days.

"The government released me, when it became clear that the disease I was afflicted with could not be diagnosed and that chances of my survival were slender." said JP.[30]

Sadhana again reported, "Mrs. Snehlata Reddy , a heroine of the president's Gold Medal winning Kannada films 'Samskar' was arrested for exacting information about Shri George Fernandes. The news of her arrest was not communicated to her husband and children. She fell sick in the prison, became serious but decline to ask for parole. Police released her only after they become cock-sure that she would die soon. She died."[31]

Mr. Lawrence Fernandes, a younger brother of George Fernandes, was arrested on 1 May 1976. He was mercilessly beaten up by the police as he described, "I was slapped by a Police officer and till three in the morning the torture continued. Even a banyan tree root was used to hit me.

"I was taken in a jeep towards the railway tracks. I screamed aloud and pleaded with the policemen not to kill me. The events of my entire life and the face of people whom I knew and loved came to mind in a flash. I know that my end was nearing.[32]

During the detention at Chandigarh prison JP's kidneys stopped functioning. No less a person than JP he suspects a kind of criminal conspiracy in it hatched by Research & Analysis Wing (RAW). It was believed that RAW was involved in such criminal activities. JP wrote in his famous letter to the people of Bihar on July 27, 1976. "I came to know of the damaged state of my kidneys only a week before my release. I did not have a kidney ailment before my arrest. Nor I was told during the four months detention in the Chandigarh that my kidneys were malfunctioning. Suddenly on November 5, 1975, I was informed that my both kidneys had stopped functioning. I could not understand how and when I became a victim of the kidney disease. I was taking all the medicines prescribed to me at Chandigarh. I was also sticking to the diet given to me in detention. So the totals collapse of my kidneys beyond my comprehensions. A number of my friends have expressed a doubt which I share that my kidneys may have deliberately damaged. The doctors at Chandigarh were nice to me. So I cannot suspect them. And no doctor (who has taken the hypocritical oath) will be a party to such a heinous crime."

"God alone knows the how my kidneys were so fatally affected. But this much is certain that I had been released only when the Indian Government was convinced that I would not survive for more than a few days." [33] J.A. Naik viewed, "In all probability his kidneys were deliberately destroyed through food or medicine and the RAW must have had some hand in it. The intelligence organization like the RAW conceiving could not have done this crime of attempting to kill JP on the orders of some officials. There must be some involvement of a politician involved in such a crime cannot be low ranking one." [34]

Indira Gandhi's father and grandfather were both lawyers, Motilal Nehru greatly more eminent than his son, Jawaharlal Nehru. But she was totally innocent of matters legal and constitutional, and was content to go by the advice of "trusted experts". On the issue of Emergency, Mr. Siddhartha Shankar Ray, then Chief Minister of West Bengal was her only legal "guide". From all accounts, he never told her that something that may be technically legal could yet be illegitimate. Why her legendary political instinct failed to warn her of this is more surprising. Maybe the objective of staying on in power was so overriding that nothing else mattered. Though there is no official acceptance of such a crime by the government but the available evidences and sources are sufficient to explore the cruel and inhuman acts of police and intelligence agencies. The Emergency regime's contention was simple, if also brutal. There was absolutely no remedy available, under Article 21 or any other, to that in preventive detention even if they were put behind bars through an order made in bad faith because all fundamental rights were suspended for the duration. When told that in addition to the Constitutional provisions, there was such a thing as the "rule of law", the Attorney-General, Niren De, argued that the rule of law existed "only within the four corners of the Constitution; natural rights did not exist outside it".

Thereupon Mr. Justice H. R. Khanna put it to him that since Article 21 guaranteed both life and liberty, surely it could not be suggested that there would be no remedy if a policeman chose to shoot a citizen. The Attorney-General replied: "Consistent with my position, My Lord, not so long as the Emergency lasts. It shocks my conscience, it may shock yours, but there is no remedy".

Despite this chilling exchange, four of the five judges upheld the Government's position; only Justice Khanna dissented. To add insult to injury, one of the four judges, Mr. M. H. Beg, made the oft-quoted remark that was as fatuous as it was gratuitous. "We understand," he wrote, "that the care and concern bestowed by the State authorities upon the welfare of the detenus who are well-housed, well-fed and well-treated, is almost maternal". Later, Mr. Beg became the Chief Justice.

Such distinguished and respected experts on Indian affairs as the late Myron Weiner have written that the Emergency was "popular" with the civil servants because it had greatly enhanced their powers. This is only partially true and basically a misreading of a rather complex situation. Another American scholar who has also studied the role of the civil service during the Emergency, Dr. Stanley H. Heginbotham, has come to the contrary conclusion that the "new regime struck more directly at the interests of the civil service". About "early retirements" of civil servants, especially in Andhra Pradesh, he noted that those "forced out because of inefficiency and dubious integrity" were, in fact, "singled out because of their lack of enthusiasm for the Emergency regime". Kuldeep Nair, eminent journalist and academicians, was arrested and kept in Tihar jail. There he faced many problems, he recalls, "110 arrested professors were kept in a cell which was for 20 persons only. There were two toilets without flesh for 110 prisoners. There was no door in the room. Rain showers came inside." Further he says, "Professor Dharmara of Rajdhani College was with us. He got admitted in the hospital of jail in the name of disease. He thought that he will get bail and will be set free. Next day we were surprised to see him again in his cell. He described the incidents which he faced. He met with old cruel prisoners in the hospital and there he viewed homosexuality which shook him."35

Keeping all the facts in mind regarding cruel and inhuman acts of police and intelligence agencies, it can be said that the police and administration was no less cruel at the time of Emergency than the British administration in India before independence.

Baroda Dynamite Case

Baroda dynamite case was related with George Fernandes, a political leader who opposed wholeheartedly the imposition of Emergency by the Indira Gandhi Government. India's premier intelligence agency Central Bureau of Intelligence (CBI) charged Mr. Fernandes and others on charges of smuggling dynamite to blow up government offices and railway tracks in protest against the imposition of Emergency by Indira Gandhi regime. He along with his comrades was also charged with waging war against the Indian state to overthrow the political establishment.

George Fernandes during Emergency arrest

The accused in this case were arrested in June 1976 and imprisoned. Fernandes was seen as the key conspirator in the case. He emerged as a figurehead of resistance against the autocratic regime of Indira Gandhi. Other associates of Fernandes, charged in this case were, Viren J. Shah, Madhu Limaye, M.S.Apparao, Madhu Dandhavate, Snehlata Reddy and others. George Fernandes later on claimed that Mr. M.Karunanidhi, the chief of Dravid Munetra Kardgam (DMK), gave him assistance and shelter during this time.

This case against Fernandes and others was tried in Delhi as Central Bureau of Investigation (CBI) justified that though the site of the incident was Baroda, the case had national ramifications.

George Fernandes contested the Lok Sabha elections of 1977 from Muzaffarpur in Bihar, while he was in jail under trail in this case. His supporters campaigned with his photo in prison cage and chains. Public expressed faith in his leadership and he won the election. A new government led by Janata Party came into power at the centre after the elections and the case against Fernandes and others was dropped and all the accused were released.

Should Guilty Men be Forgiven and Forgotten?

The unconstitutional and illegitimate excesses and torture done by the government officials on the orders of their political lords during Emergency era were inhuman and they made an irreplaceable memory on those unfortunate men and women who bore such cruelties. All such torturous acts were done by the government machinery from the inspiration of political bosses. Very often in a developing society like India which got independence after a long freedom struggle, democratic institutions and democracy as such was in a phase of development during this time. Government officials behave as a member of closed elite group based on caste, religion or sectarian lines. They are more loyal to their political bosses than their duties and responsibilities. According to J.A. Naik, the most horrible episodes and incidents in history should not be forgotten a forgiven if we were to build up healthy social and political traditions and strengthen the roots of political system. If we were to strengthen the roots of democracy in India, it will be short-sighted on our part to forget and forgive the Emergency episode." Further he said, "The enormous historic significance of creating a tradition of public opinion against the Emergency episode should not be overlooked. By reminding the people in a traditional and institutional manner of what had happened during the Emergency and what would have happened to the people and the country under the dynastic rule, we may strengthen the roots of democracy."

"It is not a question of doing political witch-hunting; it is a question of strengthening the roots of justice in society. An Englishman by name Guy Fawkes had plotted to dynamite British Parliament

House in 1605. Still the anniversary of that Gunpowder Plot is celebrated every year in England and his acts are condemned in public meetings and a symbolic search of Parliament House is made at night. This is done not to do any political witch-hunting but to strengthen the political institution."

"The international community is still hunting for the associates of Hitler and Adolph Eichmanns are sent to prison in their old age. This is not done because of any sense of victimization against somebody. It is done with a view to punishing the criminals, meeting the ends of justice, and building up a healthy tradition against crimes against humanity."[36]

Role of Administration during Emergency

To be sure, there was no death of civil servants, senior and junior, who bent over backwards to do the bidding of the Emergency regime with even greater zeal than was expected of them. With an eye on the main chance, many of them ingratiated themselves with Sanjay Gandhi, accurately perceived as the fountainhead of authority. But the number of these zealots, proportionate to the size of the bureaucracy, was relatively small, perhaps 15 to 20 per cent.

An equal percentage of civil servants, resentful of the Emergency and conscious of the standards expected of them, quietly tried to mitigate the Emergency's crudities as best they could. The mass of bureaucrats in between was content to coast along with the prevailing wind, rationalizing its attitude by invoking the bureaucratic imperative of obeying the law and lawful orders. There is no doubt, however, that the Emergency had the most damaging and dangerous, effect of politicizing the civil services down the line and destroying whatever cohesion and esprit de corps had existed earlier. Sadly, this malaise, like several other pernicious legacies of the Emergency era such as arbitrary arrests, torture, custodial deaths, has worsened since then. The situation in the States may be more appalling but it is bad enough at the Centre. Nor is anyone trying to do anything about it.

Politicization and degeneration of the police and Para-military forces have surpassed even the havoc played with the civil services. These, particularly the Border Security Force (BSF), and the Central Reserve Police Force (CRPF) were Indira Gandhi's main instruments for making the Emergency tick. But as a result of the "accountability" that followed during the Janata regime and subsequent developments, including the prolonged involvement of the Central Police Organizations in countering insurgency, they are very badly run down. If the present or any future Government is foolish enough to want to take recourse to Emergency, it will find that it has no instrument left to enforce it?

Shah Commission

"Mr. Justice J. C. Shah, who was asked to inquire into the Emergency, has painstakingly recorded all this and more. However, the trouble with the Shah Commission's three reports is best described in the words of Mr. Arun Shourie, the well-known crusading journalist who has never been an admirer of Indira Gandhi's and later on became a Minister in Atal Bihari Vajpayee led Government. When the Shah Commission was about to submit its third and final report, Mr. Shourie wrote that it "was ending its tenure on a sad note. By now it has become an embarrassment - not to Mrs. Gandhi but to the Janata Government."

To cut a long story short, it was the Janata Government that, because of its incompetence, constant internecine quarrels that eventually led to its ignominious collapse and its manic persecution of Indira Gandhi, that made the country forget the Emergency and start praying for her return to power. And return to power she did in just about a 1,000 days after she was supposed to have been, in Mr. Atal Behari Vajpayee's words, "consigned to the dustbin of history"[37]

Emergency is though seen as direct assault on our democracy but it produced some positive effects also. Many people at the time of Emergency felt relieved with the restoration of Public order and discipline and thought that the country had been saved from the disorder and chaos. There was decrease in the crime (though crimes committed by

Police and Administration against humanity reached at its zenith), gheraos controlled, demonstrations came to an end, there was calm and tranquility on the campuses. Inder Malhotra, a journalist wrote, "The return of normal and orderly life, after relentless disruption by strikes protest marches, sit-ins and clashes with the Police, was applauded by most people. In its initial months at least, the Emergency restored to India a kind of calm it had not known for years."[38]

There was discipline in administration regarding punctuality with government servants coming to office on time. Quick, dramatic and well-published action was taken against smugglers, hoarders, blackmarketeers, illegal traders in foreign currency and tax evaders, with several thousands of them were put behind bars under MISA (Maintenance of Internal Security Act).

Not only did the J.P. movement turn into a pricked balloon as soon as Indira Gandhi did act, but also a surprisingly large number of people, not particularly sympathetic to the Prime Minister, welcomed the Emergency during its initial phase at least. Their relief over the return of normal life after the almost daily chaos caused by unending marches, rallies, strikes, sit-ins and so on was genuine. This feeling was reinforced when Government employees started taking their work seriously and fewer tea breaks. The more foolish of Indira Gandhi's spin doctors, anxious to publicise the "gains of the Emergency", even started bragging that the trains were running on time!

There was a major improvement in economy, through only some it was really due to steps taken under the Emergency; some of it being the result of excellent rains and some of the policies initiated much before the emergency. Price situation improved due the availability of essential including foodstuffs.

Twenty point programme was announced by the prime minister on 1 July which aroused hopes among public as its edge was the socio-economic uplift of the vast masses of the rural poor. The programme promised to liquidate the existing debt of landless labors, small farmers and rural artisans and extend alternate credit to them, abolish bonded labor, implement the exiting agricultural land ceiling laws and distribute surplus land to land less, provide house sites to landless labourers and weaker sections, revise upward minimum wages of agricultural labor, provide special help to handloom industry, bring down prices, prevent tax evasion and smuggling, increase production streamline distribution of essential commodities, increase the limit of income tax exemption to Rs 8000, and liberalized investment procedures. Some progress was made in implementing this programme.

Bonded labor was declared illegal but very little was done in practice. Minimum usages for agricultural labors were enhanced but their enforcement was tardy. Laws were passed in different states placing a moratorium on the recovery of debt from the landless labours and small farmers and in some cases to scale down or liquidate their debts. But the scale of the alternate credit provided through nationalized banks and rural co-operative institution was small and dependence on the usurious moneylenders, who were often also big land owners, remained. The rural segment of the twenty point programme ran out of steam as its progress was hindered by large landowner and rich peasant and an unsympathetic bureaucracy. As a whole the programme brought some relief to the rural poor, there was little improvement in their basic condition.

Though Emergency maintained some discipline in the government's offices and administration official remained unresponsive to public and could not change their attitude towards public rather they got more teethes in the forms of rigorous laws under Emergency to harass the innocents. Slogans like Batein Kam, Kaam Zyada (Talk less, Work more) contributed in the increased production but this also created a kind of fear amongst workers as it was a negative motivational method.

Though Emergency gave minute contributions in the form of increased production and law and order but it was the cost of much bigger values of democracy. It can be said that the demerits of the emergency are more significant the merits.

Was Emergency inevitable?

Now the question arises whether proclamation of Emergency was necessary or not. Prime Minister Indira Gandhi justified her action of imposing

Emergency in terms of National, political interest and primarily on three grounds. First, India's stability, security, integrity and democracy were in danger from the disruptive character of the JP movement. Referring to JP's speeches, she accused the opposition if inciting the armed forces to mutiny and the police to rebel. Second, there was need to implement a programme of rapid economic development in the interest of the poor and the under privileged. Third, she warned against intervention and subversion from abroad with the aim of weakling and destabilizing India.

But contrary to her few contemporary political and non- political figures viewed her action of imposing Emergency as a step ahead in the direction of imposing dynastic rule in India and taking all the powers in hands.

Few writers view that it was best option for India Gandhi at that moment to step down and wait for the final verdict of the court. After that she could have contested election to come again in the power. Inder Malhotra observes "After this verdict, particularly after the conditional stay granted by the apex court, the best course open to her was gracefully to step down temporarily and return to her high office after winning her appeal against the judgment. There was hardly any chance of the apex court upholding the High Court verdict because the offences of which she was "convicted" were trivial and technical. According to James Cameron in The Guardian, it was "as though a head of government should go to the block for a parking ticket". Back home, however, hardly anyone was willing to concede this. Anti-Indira sentiment was at a crescendo. The cry across the land was that she must quit."[39]

The unabashedly personal motivation behind the Emergency's imposition had a symbiotic relationship with an equally unashamed drive to ensure dynastic succession. Within a few months of the June 25 hammer blow, Sanjay Gandhi had been well and truly anointed as the "heir apparent". It is arguable that this would not have been possible without the Emergency. His ways were rude and crude. He had a knack of attracting riff-raff and roughnecks to him. But none of this prevented Congressmen, high and low, from fawning on him and swearing "eternal loyalty" to his mother and her family. No wonder, Prof. Rajni Kothari wrote that for Indira Gandhi, the Emergency was "an instrument for personal survival and family aggrandizement". Sanjay died within months of his mother's triumphant return to power in 1980, but the cult of the dynasty lives on.

Few days after the Allahabad High Court verdict which came against Indira Gandhi, on 20th June 1975 a very mammoth rally was held at Boat Club ground in New Delhi. The press described it as the biggest ever held rally in the capital and according to some estimates not less than ten lakhs persons were brought to it. People from all over India were brought to New Delhi by special trains, cars and trucks for this huge gathering which was to demonstrate its support to Prime Minister Indira Gandhi. According to press reports about 7000 cars and more than 4000 trucks plied between the Punjab, Haryana and New Delhi to bring Mrs. Indira Gandhi's supporters to the capital. Many crore rupees must have been spent on it. Very few people in Delhi took this rally seriously because such meetings had become familiar sight in New Delhi in those days.

It was a totally different rally as for the first time in independent India's history all members of the Prime Minister's family sat on the stage, and Prime Minister Indira Gandhi addressed the mammoth gathering. Except the congress president, no non-Nehru clan member was allowed on the dais and he gave his lives briefest speech of two and a half minutes. All others leaders were with their state contingents. On the dais Mrs. Indira Gandhi, Sanjay Gandhi, Rajiv Gandhi and Rajiv's wife. Sanjay's wife was conspicuously absent.

J.K. Naik observed the situation, "Some Delhi papers expressed a little surprise over such a family 'family gathering' but nobody could foresee its significance. The significance was unmistakable. The Prime Minister had announced to the people of India and rest of the world that now onwards the members of the Nehru family would rule over India. This meeting was the symbolic message. This meeting was held only for conveying this very massage to the masses of India and their leaders."

He further says, "At this point Mr. Sanjay Gandhi gradually got hold over government and the administration. His influence increased over Mrs. Gandhi as she herself revealed at a letter stage that Sanjay came to her rescue after the verdict of Allahabad High court and protected her. When Sanjay threw him in the role of her mother protector some of her colleagues, on her own account, were suspected and were not trust worthy. She developed this feeling of trusting her son more than anybody else during this crucial period when her political career and future was rudely shocked by the Allahabad verdict and this psychological aspect, her own feeling about her son and the colleagues must have had its own impact dynastic dictatorship in the country and proclaims the Emergency with this view."[40]

Was Emergency imposed due to the JP's call to armed forces not to obey the illegal orders or to the Satyagrah plan of the opposition? As Bipan Chandra sees some justification in it "The agitation methods adopted and propagated by the JP movement were also extra- constitutional and undemocratic". He further says "more serious was JP's incitement to the army, police and civil services to rebel. Several times during the course of the movement, he urged them not to obey orders that were 'unjust' and beyond the call of duty or 'illegal and unjust' or 'unconstitutional, illegal or against their conscience".

"The opposition plan had all the hallmarks of a coup d'état." writes Chandra. He further said, "The danger of authoritarianism did not come from JP who was not planning or giving direction to an authoritarian coup d'état. But there were, others around him who were so inclined who were increasingly coming to control the movement and who could not capitalize basically weak personality."[41]Thus indirectly he supported the act of imposing Emergency on the pretext of JP's call to armed forces and police.

But some others like J.A. Naik contrast this opinion. According to him, "the Emergency had very little, if any, to do with JP movement or his call to armed forces not to obey the illegal orders or to the Satyagrah plan of the opposition. It was a sudden development following the Allahabad High court judgment removing her from the seat of power. Had there been no Allahabad High court Judgment probably the Emergency would not have come soon and might not have been executed so ruthlessly."

"Why had dictatorship became inevitable to her? It had become inevitable because political power was slipping from his hands and she had no ways of meeting such a challenge democratically. She indulged into non- democratic methods and power was retained in the preceding few years with the help of a secret police organization that had indulged into a planned criminal activity." Further he adds, "The doings of Research & Analysis wing of the Prime Minister's secretariat undoubtedly had some share in compelling Mrs. Gandhi to retain political power at all costs and by any means. There was a very strong suspicion of the involvement of the RAW in the murder of L.N. Mishra, Nagarmala and Kashyap.The RAW was suspected to have planted bombs in the cars of chief justice of the Supreme Court." "The government had developed the murderer's mentality. Once the criminal commits a murder, he does look back in committing the subsequent one for the purpose of destroying the evidences of the first and prolonging the course. The head of secret police organization had to the price of their lives at same stage."[42]

The second major question about the Emergency, to which no satisfactory answer is available even a quarter of a century later, revolves around the immediate reaction to Emergency or rather the utter lack of it. For over a year, India had reverberated with the war cries of those who said that since Indira Gandhi was "destroying democracy", they were determined to "fight her to the finish". But when the blow actually fell and it looked as if democracy had been destroyed, there was not even a squeak, leave alone resistance, anywhere in this vast land.

As they say, not a dog barked. The Emergency's apparent acceptance was no less stunning than its abrupt proclamation. Many people were, of course, sullen. In private, they expressed their frustration and anger, but in public they went about their jobs as if nothing had happened. On the other hand, there was no dearth of those only too happy to jump on the Emergency's bandwagon. Some of these worthies had only a few weeks earlier ostentatiously joined J.P.'s famous "march on Parliament".

Who was ruling?

Indira or Sanjay? Existing evidences show that Sanjay Gandhi had established himself as a defector ruler in the last of June though he started figuring in the press and on the AIR from September onwards. Mrs. Lewis Simons, a correspondent of Washington Post, who was the first foreign correspondent to be expelled from India after the proclamation of Emergency, wrote a sensational piece in the July in which he had maintained that Sanjay Gandhi had already emerged as the successor of the Prime Minister and he was ruling over India from her residence. He revealed that he was very aggressive towards his mother from childhood and he was a sort of a non-controllable boy since his father's death. He had slapped his mother at a family dinner in the presence of others. This article was banned in India. It was made a sensational hit in the international press and was widely reproduced.

These all evidences show that Sanjay Gandhi was able to influence Prime Minister Indira Gandhi's very action. J.K. Naik gives other examples which show the influence of Sanjay Gandhi in Government. "Rajasthan's chief minister Hardeo Joshi had gone to Delhi in the first week of July and wanted to see Indira Gandhi. He was asked to see Sanjay Gandhi and discuss his problems with him. He was baffled, as some others in the court. He saw Sanjay and took his directions."[43] Sanjay Gandhi became a closest associate of Prime Minister Indira Gandhi and it was believed that he was in a position to influence her each and every decision. Perhaps Indira Gandhi became was feeling so insecure in those days that she was suspicious everyone and Sanjay Gandhi became a man on whom she could rely due to her blood relationship. Further Sanjay utilized this intimate relationship with her mother to strengthen his own political stature.

Sanjay Gandhi: a very intimate advisor

Within a fortnight after the imposition of Emergency Mrs. Gandhi got the constitution amended for placing her election, along with that of the president, beyond the security of judiciary.

The very following days another constitutional amendment (41st) was adopted which extended immunity from criminal and civil proceedings to her. Her involvement in the criminal doings of the RAW was uppermost in her mind when she proclaimed Emergency. This is indicated by the close examination of the existing evidences.

References

1. Inder Malhotra, The Hindu, June 25, 2000
2. *Ibid.*
3. Austin, Granville, *Working a Democratic Constitution: A History of the Indian Experience*, (New Delhi, Oxford University Press, 2000) p.
4. Inder Malhotra, The Hindu, June 25th, 2000
5. *Ibid.*
6. *Ibid.*
7. *Ibid.*
8. Morarji Desai to Oriana Fallaci, *New Republic* quoted in Francine R. Frankel, *India's Political Economy 1947-1977* : The Gradual Revolution (Princeton: Princeton University Press,1978) p.544
9. Bipan Chandra, et.al. (ed.), *India After Independence1947-2000,* (New Delhi: Penguin Books,2000) p.246
10. The Times Of India, (7 March 1975)
11. Inder Malhotra, The Hindu, June 25th, 2000

12. Naik, J.A. *An alternative Polity for India*, (New Delhi: S.chand & Company Ltd., March 1976) p.14

13. Chandra Bipan, et.al. (ed.), *India After Independence1947-2000*, (New Delhi: Penguin Books, 2000) p.248

14. Ibid. p.248

15. Samved

16. Bhattacharjea, Ajit, *Jay Prakash Narayan; A Political Biography*, (Noida: Vikas Publishing House Pvt.Ltd.,1975) pp.143-144

17. The times of India, March 7,1975

18. Bhattacharjea, Ajit, *Jay Prakash Narayan: A Political Biography*, (Noida: Vikas publishing house Pvt.Ltd.,1975) p.141

19. The Times of India, March 7,1975

20. Ibid

21. Prasad, Bimal (ed.), *A Revolutionary's Quest: Selected Writings Of Jaya Prakash Narayan* (New Delhi: Oxford University Press, 1980) p.388

22. Prasad, Bimal et.al. (ed.), *Jaya Prakash NarayanEssential writings 1929-1979 A Centenary Volume (1902-2002)* (Delhi: Konark Publishers Pvt. Ltd, 2002) p.44

23. Morarji Desai to Oriana Fallaci, *New Republic* quoted in Francine R. Frankel, *India's Political Economy 1947-1977*,(Princeton: Princeton University Press, 1978)p.544

24. Mehta, Ved, *A Family Affair: India Under Three Prime Ministers* (Delhi: Oxford University Press,1982)

25. Frank, Katherine, *Indira: The life of Indira Nehru Gandhi* (Boston: Houghton Mifflin Hartcourt, 2002)

26. Inder Malhotra, The Hindu, June 25th, 2000

27. The Times of India, March 4, 1977

28. Sadhana, February 8, 1977

29. Sadhana, March 27, 1976

30. Inder Malhotra, The Hindu, June 25, 2000

31. Indian Express, February 26, 1977

32. Sadhana, March 5, 1977, p.2

33. The Times of India, March 23rd, 1977, p.4

34. Indian Express, Feb 26, 1977

35. Naik, J.A., *The Great Janata Revolution*, (New Delhi: S.Chand & Company, 1977) p.27

36. Kuldeep Nair, Sangrah Times, November 2006, pp.55-56

37. Naik, J.A., *The Great Janata Revolution*, (New Delhi: S.Chand & Company, 1977) pp.28-29-30

38. Inder Malhotra, The Hindu, June 25th, 2000

39. Inder Malhotra, Seminar, March 1977, New Delhi

40. Inder Malhotra, The Hindu, June 25th, 2000

41. Naik, J.A., *The Great Janata Revolution*, (New Delhi: S.Chand & Company, 1977) p.15

42. Chandra, Bipan, et.al. (ed.), *India after Independence1947- 2000*, (New Delhi: Penguin Books, 2000), pp.251-252

43. Naik, J.A., The *Great Janata Revolution*, (New Delhi: S.Chand & Company, 1977) pp.17-18

44. Ibid. p.20

NON - CONGRESS GOVERNMENT
AND CONTEMPORARY INDIAN POLITICS

Janata Government

Janata Government came into power after the elections held just after Emergency in 1977. It was the first non-congress government at centre which ended the dominance of congress on Indian politics to some extent. JP was the main inspirational source of the Janata Government.

End of Emergency rule

Popular measures like twenty point program which were announced by Prime Minster Mrs. Gandhi could not sustain her popularity among the people of India because many reasons. Firstly, besides all these relief measures and students, middle classes viewed Emergency as a direct attack on their liberty and democracy. For them minor economic incentives measures to bring discipline in the administration and law and order less significant than lost of liberty and democracy.

Second reason was that economic growth of first year of the Emergency could not sustain. Agricultural output declined, prices rose by ten per cent by the end of 1976. The corrupt, black marketers and smugglers resumed their activities as the shock of the Emergency wore off. The poor were unhappy with slow progress in their welfare and workers were unhappy because of limits on wages, bonus and dearness allowances and restrictions on the right to strike. The government servants and teachers were angry because they were being disciplined in their work places and in many cases were being forced to fulfill sterilization quotas.

Though progress was made but it was only on the paper and very less happened in reality. Government failed to create any new agency of social change. For the implementation of the Twenty Point Program and other developmental works, government had the machinery of old corrupt and inefficient bureaucracy. Matters took a turn for the worse because the people had no other mechanism for the voicing and redresser of their grievances.

Not only intellectuals and political workers but even a common man lived in an atmosphere of fear and insecurity. The Police and administration got not only increased power that was unchecked by criticism and exposure from the press, courts, political parties and popular movements. The drastic press censorship and the silencing of protest led to the government being kept in complete ignorance of what was happening in the country. On the other hand people knew that what appeared in the press or on the Radio was heavily censored, they no longer trusted them.

People began to feel the demerits of Emergency as it began to impact their daily lives in the form of harassment and corruption by the petty officials. Delay in lifting the Emergency created fear among the people that the authoritarian structure of the rule might be made permanent or continue for a long time because Mrs. Gandhi had got Parliament's permission to postpone elections by one year in November, 1976.The 42nd amendment of the constitution was viewed as an effort to subvert democracy by changing the very basic structure of the Constitution.

Emergence of Sanjay Gandhi as an extra-constitutional centre of power and his interference in every government order and in daily administration feared the people very much.

Moreover, the moral pressure created by the opposition leaders who were arrested and kept in prisons, defeated Indira Gandhi Psychologically as she was under huge pressure and her every action which she was taking was to justify the previous one. Bipan Chandra writes, "Under these pressures Prime Minister Indira Gandhi suddenly on 18 January, 1977, announced that elections to Lok Sabha would be held in March. She released political prisoners, lifted press censorship and other restrictions on political activities such as holding of public meetings. Political parties were allowed to campaign freely."[1]

Marry C. Carras, biographer of Indira Gandhi, viewed this action as an expression of her commitment to liberal democracy and democratic values. He argued, "Throughout her life her self-image and been that of a democrat; indeed herself respect derives in good part from his self-image......she was compelled to prove to the world and, above all, to herself, that she is and always has been a democrat."[2]

Some other writers opined that once Mrs. Gandhi became aware of the Emergency excesses and realized that the matters were getting out of her control, she decided to come out from this trap by holding elections even though it meant losing of power.

Another view is that intelligence agencies convinced her that she would win the elections. She hoped to vindicate the Emergency by winning the elections and clear way for Sanjay Gandhi to succeed her. Another view to the issue is that Mrs. Gandhi realized that the policies of Emergency had to be legitimized further through elections. She must have realized that the Emergency regime was increasingly getting discredited. She planned for greater legitimacy and political authority acquired by changing back to a democratic system. Because increasing ruthlessness and brutality in suppressing dissent would not work in a country of India's size and diversity and also in view of its democratic traditions.

The lifting of the Emergency and the elections of 1977 and their results were defining moment in India's post independence history. The election results revealed the Indian's underlying attachment to democratic values which were in turn the result of the impact of the freedom struggle and the experience of democratic functioning, including free elections since 1947. Tariq Ali has rightly said about the elections of 1977, "the urban and rural poor demonstrated in a very concrete and striking fashion that questions of basic civil rights were not merely the preoccupations of the urban middle classes."[3]

Inder Malhotra, who was covering the election campaign reported of 'truly remarkable' manner in which 'village audience' in the remote country side react to sophisticated argument about civil liberties, fundamental rights and independence of the judiciary.'[4]

Elections of 1977

After coming out from the jails, opposition leaders announced the merger of Congress (o), Jan Sangh, Bartiya Lok Dal (BLD) and socialist party into the newly formed Janata Party. Congress suffered a political blow at this moment by sudden defection from it on 2nd February 1977. JagJivan Ram, H.N. Bahuguna and Nandini Satpathi formed a new party Congress for Democracy (CFD) splitting from the Congress Party. Along with DMK, Akali Dal and CPM it formed a common front with the Janata

Party in order to give a straight fight to Congress and its allies, the CPI and AIADMK in the March election to the Lok Sabha.

The opposition Janata Front made the Emergency excesses, especially forced sterilization and the restriction of civil liberties, the major issues in their election campaign. The people also treated the elections as a referendum on the Emergency. With the popular upsurge in favor of them, the Janata Party and its allies were victorious with 330 out of 542 seats. Congress got 154 seats with CPI its ally getting 7 and the AIADMK 21 seats. Congress was completely wiped out in North India as it won only 2 seats out of 234 seats in seven northern states. Both Indira and Sanjay Gandhi lost their seats. Whereas in South India Congress improved winning 92 seats in place of 70 in 1971. The reason was that in South India, the pro-poor measures of the Twenty Point Programme were better implemented. Janata won only 6 seats in the four Southern states. The electoral verdict was mixed in Western states.

In the elections of1977 JP's contribution for Janata Party was such a great that no leader except he had such a great appeal among the masses. "Even through crippled by ill- health and dependent on the dialysis thrice a week, JP made single contribution to the resounding victory of the Janata party in the elections. He went round the round the whole country, identifying himself wholly with the Janata Party and formulating the sole issue in the elections as a choice between dictatorship and democracy"[5] writes Bimal Prasad.

The Janata Government

JP also took the opportunity to place before the people the broad outlines of his vision of a new social order for which the Janata Party was committed to work. The resounding victory of the Janata Party in the election, the selection of Morarji Desai as the leader of its Parliamentary party at the instance of JP(working with J.B.Kriplani) and the formation of a Janata Party Government at the centre led to the restoration of democracy in the country."[6]writes Bimal Prasad.

There was a crisis over the issue of Prime Minister Ship between the three aspirants, Moraji Desai, Charan Singh and Jagjivan Ram. But at the end JP ruled in favor of Morarji Desai, who was sworn in the prime Minster on 23 March. Morarji Desai headed the four parties Janata Government for about two years. Though technically it was not a coalition because its four constituents had agreed to merge and contest the elections on a single Manifesto and on a shared symbol. But the power struggle within the coalition Government was muted at the time of the formation of the Council of Ministers. The coalition Parties were represented in the government in proportion to the strength of constituent groups within the Janata Party. Even on the governing of North Indian states, a power struggle broke out between the two strongest Janata Party constituents, the Bhartiya Lok Dal (BLD), and the Jan Sangh. The BLD got

Haryana, Himachal Pradesh, Orissa and Bihar; the Jan Sangh got Rajasthan, MP and Delhi.

The newly formed Janata govt. dismissed nine congressed ruled states governments and paved the way for fresh elections to their assemblies. Assembly elections need in June 1977 in which Janata and its allies came out victorious in these states except in Tamil Nadu where AIADMK won. In West Bengal, the CPM, a Janata alloy gained an absolute majority. Control over both the parliament and states assemblies' enabled the Janata party to elect unopposed its own candidate, N. Sanjeeva Reddy, as the President of the Union in July'1977.

The Janata government immediately took step to disseminate the authoritarian features of the emergency regime and restore liberal democracy. It restored fundamental rights and full civil liberties to the press, political parties and the individuals. Through the 44th constitutional amendment 42nd amendment was modified which passed during Emergency repealing those of its provisions which has distorted the constitution. The rights of the Supreme Court to decide on the validity of central or state legislation were restored.

'Food for Work' programme was launched by the Janata government in order to provide employed. This programmed improved village infrastructure such as roads, school buildings etc., and programme was implanted efficiently by the

CPM govt. in the West Bengal.

The new government failed to take any radical steps in the direction of making JP's dream a reality. When the new government took office JP was full of ideas on how the Janata government should function in order to serve the people and usher in radical social changes based on the principles of Gandhian socialism. But hardly any senior leaded in the government seemed to have much use for such ideas. The senior members of the government called him only on rare occasions. Kuldeep Nayar writes, "I visited Prime Minister Morarji Desai and complained that JP is feeling himself neglected by the government. Morarji became angry and said, was he willing that I should visit him? You know, I never went to visit Gandhi ji, he is not greater than Gandhi."[7]

Morarji Desai

Though some of the younger leaders of the Janata party as well as the members of the Union cabinet continued to call on him from time to time but mainly to ask about his health, they seldom met him, either singly or in a group to seek his advice or guidance as to how to run the party or government to fulfill his dream of Total Revolution. On one or two occasions when JP offered some advice on his own initiative such advice was ignored completely.

The leader in the govt. were busy in their own matters of capturing more and more power and they had no time for the people or for the ideas of JP. Kuldeep Nayar writes, "Janata govt. should have taken some steps to reestablish people's confidence in law. But its leaders indulged themselves in power politics as minor personal interests. They had neither time nor interest to change the corrupt and criminal degrading system. JP wanted to separate the corrupt politician from the government."[8]

JP was unhappy at such treatment at the hands of persons whom he placed in power, what really bothered him was the failure of Janata govt. to fulfill the expectations of the people and the continued bickering amongst its leaders which finally culminated in large scale defection from the Janata Party and the fall of its govt. in July 1979. "The garden has withered away," this comment of JP revealed his deep anguish, and although he never said anything more, it was clear to everyone that he was deeply distressed by the developments leading to the tragic end of Janata govt.[9]

As stated earlier the Janata govt. leaders had little attachment to the thoughts of JP and it collapsed it own. Madhu Dandavate observes, "The Janata Party was apparently a single party, but in reality it was a combination of BLD, congress (o), Janasangh, socialist party and groups of congress dissidents led by Jagjivan Ram and H.N. Bahuguna. The Janata govt. committed to common election manifesto "Bread with freedom" had roused the hopes and aspirations of the people. But temperamental incompatibility of some leaders and fierce inner controversy over the dual membership of Janasangh (RSS and Janata Party) wrecked the Janata Party and it government. The Janata party's experiment of governance however, also revealed the desperate groups and individuals enter into a marriage of convenience for the sake of power, and their desire to maximize the benefits of power create schisms and conflicts among themselves, and these arrangements for governess ultimately collapse. The logic of raw power becomes dominant among the coopering groups to govern, but such logic is self destructive and leads to instability."[10]

Charan Singh Government

Popularly known as Chaudhary sahib among his men, Chaudhary Charan Singh was leader of Bhartiya Lok Dal. The leader of the Bharatiya Lok Dal, a major constituent of the Janata coalition, he was disappointed in his ambition to become Prime Minister in 1977 by Jayaprakash Narayan's choice of Morarji Desai. He settled at the time for the largely honorary post of Deputy Prime Minister of India. However, the internal stresses of the coalition's government caused him to leave the government with the former Lok Dal, after being promised by Mrs. Gandhi the support of the Congress Party on the floor of the House in any efforts to form a government. He was sworn in as Prime Minister with the support of just 64 MPs.

Chaudhary Charan Singh entered in Indian politics during the freedom movement of country. He was closely associated with socialist leader Dr. Ram Manohar Lohia. Charan Singh belonged to Jat community which is dominant in western Uttar Pradesh and Haryana. Being very popular within his, he derived his political strength from this particular region.

During 1857, when many Indians tried to overthrow the yoke of British slavery, one ancestor of Charan Singh, Raja Nahar Singh of Ballabhgarh (Haryana) participated in this movement very actively. Raja Nahar Singh was sent to the gallows in Chandni Chowk, Delhi. The British Indian Government after recapturing Delhi started capturing and implicating in the cases of sedition to those who were believed to be closely associated with Raja Nahar Singh. To escape from such British oppression Charan Singh's grandfather moved eastward to Bulandshahar district in Uttar Pradesh. Charan Singh was born in a village named Noorpur. His father was a farmer. Charan Singh was a good student. He did his Masters Degree in

Arts in 1925. He obtained a degree of Law the very next year.

Charan Singh was elected a member of Legislative Assembly of United Provinces (later on became Uttar Pradesh) in February 1937. He was only 34 years old at this time. He was very concerned about safeguarding the rights and welfare of farmers. He introduced an 'Agricultural Produce Market Bill' in the assembly in 1938. The Bill was intended to protect the interests of the farmers against the avarice of the traders. The Bill was published in The Hindustan Times of Delhi edition on March 31, 1938. This bill became so popular and was considered pro farmers that most of the states in India adopted this and made laws accordingly. Punjab became the first state to make law modeled on this bill in 1940.

Chaudhary Charan Singh

Chaudhary Charan Singh was a true follower of Mahatma Gandhi and his weapons of freedom struggle, 'Satyagrah and Ahimsha'. He was put behind bars many times by the British Colonial Government. He actively participated in 'Salt Satyagrah' and imprisoned for six years for breaking the 'Salt Law'. In 1940, he participated in 'Individual Satyagrah Movement' and was jailed for another one year. In August 1942, when Gandhiji waged an ultimate war against British Colonialism and started "Quit India Movement", Charan Singh jumped once again in this movement and he was jailed again by the British Indian Government under Defense of India Rules (DIR). He was released in November 1943.

When India became an independent country, Charan Singh was appointed Revenue Minister in 1952 in Uttar Pradesh Government. Being a true well-wisher of farmers, he was committed for the enforcement and implementation of the provisions of the Zamindari Abolition and Land Reforms Act. He was the major architect of this law. India cannot be a truly democratic country unless we don't work to bring socio-economic changes in our society as without giving economic freedom and equality to the deprived sections of our country, we cannot ensure the participation of each and every citizen of India in democracy. This was a common belief among many social and political observers of his time that success of Indian democracy lies in successful implementation of Land Reforms Act.

Chaudhary Charan Singh was very critical and opposed to Prime Minister Jawaharlal Nehru on his Soviet Model economic planning and reforms. Charan Singh believed that cooperative farms like Soviet Union would not succeed in Indian social system. He argued that the right of ownership was important to the farmer in remaining a cultivator. Being a son of a farmer, he understood the meaning of ownership of land for a cultivator.

Charan Singh left the Congress party and formed his own political party in1967. He became Chief Minister of Uttar Pradesh for two short tenures in 1967 and in 1970. When Prime Minister Indira Gandhi imposed Emergency on the country on June 25, 1975, Charan Singh was arrested and put behind the bars. All the leaders of opposition parties and whosoever challenged her was arrested and jailed. When Emergency was removed and general elections of Lok Sabha held, Prime Minister Indira Gandhi was voted out from the office. Public voted in favor of opposition parties and Morarji Desai became Prime Minister of India. When Morarji Desai led Government fell Charan Singh was appointed as Prime Minister of country in 1979. He was very concerned for the security of the country which was clearly visible in his speech to the nation delivered on the Independence Day, August 15, 1979. He observed Pakistan's nuclear ambition as a major threat to India.

He was very cautious and eager for the welfare of industrial labors. In his opinion Indian labor laws had to be pro labor if India were to become competitive in world economy.

Chaudhary Charan Singh as Prime Minister of India never faced Loksabha, the lower house of Indian Parliament. The day before the Lok Sabha was due to meet for the first time during the Prime Ministership of Charan Singh, Indian National Congress withdrew its support from the Charan Singh led government. The Union Government came in minority and Chaudhary Charan Singh resigned from the post of Prime Minister. Lok Sabha was dissolved and General Elections were announced.

After the fall of Morarji Desai led govt. a new coalition govt. was formed with the Mr. Charan Singh as Prime Minster in October, 1979. This coalition included leaders and groups from the entire spectrum of Indian politics, CPI, CPI (M) on the one hand and those who were close to big business groups on the other. The party headed by Mr. Charan Singh was a party of defectors and was not recognized as a party in Lok Sabha and did not enjoy absolute Majority. It was assured of outside support from the congress (I) party. However, Charan Singh tendered his resignation to the president because of the withdrawal of support by congress (I) to his govt. The Charan Singh government advised the president to dissolved the Lok Sabha which was accepted and the mid- term elections were announced.

JP was very unhappy with the incidents which

were taking place. He wrote letters to Desai and Chandra Shekhar, then president of Janata party reminding them of the promise made to the people by the Janata Party at time of the election (1977) and warning them of the serious danger that lay ahead if they were not speedily implemented.

JP fell seriously ill and was taken to the Jaslok Hospital in Bombay, which had almost become his second home since his release from prison in November 1975. There were improvement and fluctuation in JP's health. 'Once his health shattered so much that Intelligence agency informed Delhi that anything could happen anytime. This rumor spread in Delhi like fire in the jungle and Prime Minster Morarji Desai announced in the parliament, "JP is dead." The news spread in the whole world while JP was still alive. Next day Prime Minster Morarji Desai apologized before parliament for providing wrong information. There was huge anger and dissatisfaction over Prime Minster Morarji Desai's irresponsible behavior.'11

Lack of possibility of effective public activity and fast- deteriorating political situation in the country to which the various act of omission and commission by the Janata Government and increasing squabbles among its leaders had significantly contributed seemed finally to have sapped his will to live. Early on the morning of 8 October 1979, he passed away in his deep, sad and disillusioned and conscious till the end his quest had remained unfulfilled.

JP failed-?

Many people view that JP totally failed in his task of total revolution and few went far to accuse JP for his ideology. Like Bipan Chandra views, "the JP movement was flawed in many respects, in terms of both its composition and its action and character and Philosophy of its leader." He further adds, "From the early fifties he became a critic of the parliament democracy. For years, he tried to popularize the concept of 'party less democracy'. During 1974-75 he also advocated 'Total Revolution' (Sampooran Kranti). Both concepts were unclear and nebulous, and at not stage were able to delineate or even explain what a political system without political parties would involve or how would the popular will get expressed or implemented in it."[12]

But to understand the JP's success, these chances should be kept in the mind which enabled people for their greater participation in political matters. JP's efforts aroused political awareness among people and increased their desire to think and ask those political issues which were directly related to their lives and socio –economic conditions. Ravindra Bharti rightly observed, "The JP movement aroused feeling of courage amongst the rural and urban youth. Politics which was language of the rich, now even a common man was able to understand. Youth were asking questions and they became able to argue even Prime Minster Morarji Desai or any other cabinet minister. Politics came out from the Kothis and Havelis (house of rich man) and it became a part of tea stalls and for this credit goes to JP and his movement."[13]

He further adds that he gave dynamism to the static society.[14]

JP was aware of the fact that the task of total revolution is so big that it may take many years, "perhaps I will not be alive to see my dream of total revolution taking shape in practice but whenever the last man of the society shall be able to live with respect and dignity, will be able to work according to his/her capacity and will able to get accordingly', I will be satisfied."[15]

Few others viewed that JP committed some strategic mistakes in his great mission of 'Total Revolution'. Anchal Sinha writes, "JP committed many mistakes during 1975-77). He believed in Mao and Marx but he kept himself aloof from the politics, it was a major mistake. He organized "Sangharsh Vahini" in 1975 but directed it separate itself from the power, thus committing second mistake. He could not understand the tricks of political parties. In the elections of 1977 he could have directed Vahini or any other organization to contest in elections, which could have changed the whole picture but we declared old congress man Morarji Desai as Prime Minster which can be said a mistake."[16]

But as a whole it can be said that JP did not fail but actually it was failure of those leaders who were with him on and on whom he trusted very much. But they betrayed not only to JP and his 'Total Revolution' but also to the people of India for failing to complete the promise made during 1977 elections. About the question of failure of JP, eminent Journalist Ashok Bajpai comment, "Failure of few men sometimes is more inspirational and educative than the success of people. Failure of JP is much greater and valuable than the minor victories."[17]

What failure and success meant to JP, he himself spoke about it in the form a poem which he composed on 9 August 1975, while he was a prisoner at Chandigarh? This (as translated from the original in Hindi) in part runs as follows-

Different are my definitions,

Of success and failure.

What the world calls failures,

Were stages in the Quest (for a revolution?)

Those stages are innumerable,

The destination too is far off

I do not have to stop anywhere,

Whatever the road blocks on the way.

I have no ambition for myself.

Everything is decided to God,

So I am satisfied with my failures,

And this unsuccessful life

Will be blessed a hundred times.

If for the dear young fellow- seekers

It makes the thorny path a bit easy.[18]

Coalition government of 1989 led by Vishwanath Pratap Singh

Entering local politics in Allahabad in the Nehru era, V.P. Singh soon made a name for himself in the state Congress Party for his unfailing rectitude, a reputation that he would carry with him throughout his career.

He was handpicked by Indira Gandhi to serve as the Chief Minister of Uttar Pradesh in 1980, when the Congress came back to power after the Janata interregnum. As CM, he cracked down hard on the dacoity, or banditry, problem that was particularly severe in the rural districts of the south-west. He received much favorable national publicity when he offered to resign following a self-professed failure to stamp out the problem, and again when he personally oversaw the surrender of some of the most feared dacoits of the area in 1983.

Following Rajiv Gandhi's massive mandate in the 1984 General elections, he was appointed to the crucial post of Finance Minister, where he oversaw the gradual relaxation of the license Raj that Rajiv had in mind. He also gave extra power to the Enforcement Directorate of the Finance Ministry, which is the wing of the ministry charged with tracking down tax evaders. Following a number of high-profile raids on suspected evaders - including Dhirubhai Ambani - Rajiv was forced to sack him as Finance Minister, possibly because many of the raids were conducted on industrialists who had supported the Congress financially in the past. However, Singh's popularity was at such a pitch now that only a sideways move was possible, to the Defense Ministry.

Once ensconced in North Block, Singh began to investigate the notoriously murky world of defense procurement. After a while, word began to spread that Singh possessed information about the Bofors defense deal that could damage the Prime Minister's reputation. Before he could act on it, he was dismissed from the Cabinet and, in response, resigned his memberships in the Congress Party and the Lok Sabha.

Together with associates Arun Nehru and Arif Mohammed Khan, Singh floated an opposition party named the Jan Morcha. He was re-elected to Lok Sabha in a bye-election from Allahabad defeating Anil Shastri. On 11 October 1988, the birthday of the original Janata coalition's spiritual leader Jayaprakash Narayan, the Janata Dal was formed by merger of Jan Morcha, Janata Party, Lok Dal and Congress (S), in order to bring together all the centrist parties opposed to the Rajiv Gandhi government.

The Janata Dal fought the elections in 1989 after coming to an agreement with the right-wing Bharatiya Janata Party and the Communist Left Front that served to unify the anti-Congress vote under the banner of a grouping called the National Front. The three Opposition groupings earned a simple majority in the Lok Sabha and decided to form a government. The Communists and the BJP refused to serve in the government, preferring to support it from outside.

In a dramatic meeting in the Central Hall of Parliament on the 1st of December, V.P Singh proposed the name of Devi Lal as Prime Minister, in spite of the fact that he himself had been clearly projected by the anti-Congress forces as the 'clean' alternative to Rajiv and their Prime Ministerial candidate. Devi Lal, a Jat leader from Haryana stood up and refused the nomination, and said that he would prefer to be an 'elder uncle' to the Government, and that Singh should be PM. This last part came as a clear surprise to Chandra Shekhar, the former head of the erstwhile Janata Party, and Singh's greatest rival within the Janata Dal. Shekhar, who had clearly expected that an agreement had been forged with Lal as the consensus candidate, stormed out of the meeting and refused to serve in the Cabinet.

Singh held office for slightly less than a year, from December 2, 1989 - November 10, 1990.He faced his first crisis within few days of taking office: terrorists kidnapped the daughter of his Home Minister, Mufti Mohammad Sayeed (Ex Chief Minister of Jammu and Kashmir. His government caved into the demand for releasing militants in exchange; partly to end the storm of criticism that followed, he shortly thereafter appointed Jagmohan, a controversial former bureaucrat, as Governor of Jammu and Kashmir, on the insistence of the BJP, who were concerned that an insufficiently hard line was being taken with the separatist element in the state. Jagmohan subsequently inflamed opinion in the Valley when he ordered troops to fire on the funeral procession of the unofficial head of Kashmiri Islam, the Mirwaiz, and shortly thereafter the Kashmir insurgency began in earnest. In contrast, in Punjab, Singh replaced the hardliner Siddhartha Shankar Ray as Governor with another former bureaucrat, Nirmal Kumar Mukarji, who moved forward on a timetable for fresh elections. Singh himself made a much-publicised visit to the Golden Temple to ask forgiveness for Operation Bluestar and the combination of events caused the long rebellion in Punjab to die down markedly in a few months. V.P. Singh withdrew the Indian Peace Keeping Force (IPKF) from Sri Lanka after he saw that Rajiv Gandhi's Sri Lanka policy was a miserable failure having cost over 1000 Indian soldiers' lives, over 5000 Sri Lankan Tamil lives and cost over 2000 crores; and the Sri Lankan leader Premadasa wanted the IPKF to leave in March 1990.

Singh himself wished to move forward nationally on social justice-related issues, which would in addition consolidate the caste coalition that supported the Janata Dal in North India, and accordingly decided to implement the recommendations of the Mandal Commission which suggested that a fixed quota of all jobs in the public sector be reserved for members of the historically disadvantaged Other Backward Class. This decision led to widespread protests among the youth in urban areas in North India.

Vishwanath Pratap Singh

Meanwhile the BJP was moving its own agenda forward: in particular, the Ram Janmabhoomi agitation, which served as a rallying cry for several radical Hindu organizations, took on new life. The party president, Lal Krishna Advani, toured the northern states on a rath - a bus converted to look like a chariot - with the intention of drumming up support. Before he could complete it, by reaching the disputed site in Ayodhya, he was arrested on Singh's orders on the charges of disturbing the peace and fomenting communal tension. This led to the BJP's suspension of support to the National Front government. V.P. Singh faced the vote of confidence with a high moral ground that he stood for secularism, that he saved the Babri Masjid at the cost of power and that basic principles were involved. But he lost the vote by 142-346.

Chandra Shekhar immediately seized the moment and left the Janata Dal with several of his own supporters to form the Samajwadi Janata Dal, or the Socialist People's Party. Although he had a mere 64 MPs, Rajiv Gandhi, the leader of the Opposition, agreed to support him on the floor of the House. He won a confidence motion and was sworn in as Prime Minister. He lasted only a few months Congress Party withdrew support and fresh elections were called.

Singh decided against contesting the new elections and retired from active politics. He spent the next few years touring the country speaking about matters related to issues of social justice, and painting. In the Deve Gowda and I.K. Gujral governments of the late 1990s, Singh acted as a sort of elder statesman and advisor for the successors to the National Front coalition. He was diagnosed with cancer in 1998 and ceased his public appearances.

When his cancer went into remission in 2003, he once again became a visible figure, especially in the many groupings that had inherited the space once occupied by his Janata Dal. Ironically, his caste-based social justice policies had caused the rise of parties like the Bahujan Samaj Party that were formed around caste identities; his own brand of populist socialism was thus squeezed out of the electoral marketplace. To remedy this, he re-formed the Jan Morcha in 2005, and began the slow process of aggregation of smaller parties in the North with a view to contesting the Uttar Pradesh vidhan Sabha elections scheduled for 2007.

Singh was placed under arrest in Ghaziabad as he and his supporters were proceeding towards a hauling where prohibitory orders under Section 144 had been imposed to join the farmers agitating against the acquisition of land by the Anil Ambani-owned Reliance Industries and demanding adequate compensation.

According to Prem Shankar Jha "Few Indian political leaders have been as reviled as V.P. Singh. Few have made as lasting a contribution to Indian nation building. I refer, of course, to his decision in August 1990 to implement the Mandal Commission's recommendations and reserve 27 per cent of the jobs in Central government for the backward classes. I was privileged to witness the paradox at close quarters. This is how it happened.

Contrary to the impression that was assiduously spread by the media, his decision was no last minute, knee-jerk attempt to shore up his shaky minority government. VP had implemented the recommendations in Uttar Pradesh when he was its chief minister in 1980. In 1989, when the National Front obtained only seven seats in the south, 81 of its 144 MPs were backward-caste members of the Janata Dal. As a result the question of not implementing Mandal simply did not arise. What was knee-jerk was VP's decision to announce the implementation of the Mandal award without any warning on August 7. For this the coming confrontation with the BJP over the Ram Janmabhoomi temple issue was mainly to blame. In the beginning of July, I was asked to join a meeting between VP and the cabinet secretary, Vinod Pande. Apparently (this was when I was not present) the government had come to know that the BJP was going to break its pre-election promise not to allow the Ram temple to become an issue in its continued support of the government. "Further he goes on to say:

"VP had called the meeting to work out a strategy for countering the threat to the government that this would pose. By then he had held around a dozen meetings with members of the Ram Janmabhoomi Nyas and the Babri Masjid Action Committee (BMAC) and had got nowhere. It had become apparent to him that the roadblock was no longer technical, but the determination by the Sangh Parivar and the BMAC to piggyback on the issue to build their bases among Hindus and Muslims.

To avoid a confrontation with the BJP, VP first pinned his hopes on squeezing a decision out of the Allahabad High Court on the cases that had been before it for 41 years. Any decision from it would have given him moral and legal foundation for forcing his ruling upon the contending parties. It would have given the BJP a fig leaf it needed to not bring down the National Front government. But the court, which had slept over the issue for years, continued to slumber.

Pandey must have reported to him sometime in July that the court was not willing to oblige.

That was when VP decided to bring forward the Mandal decision. He knew the chances of his government surviving beyond October 30 were slight. He wanted to implement this part of the programme before it fell, partly because it was covered by his 61-point action programme, and partly because it would help consolidate a base for the Janata Dal. Where he went wrong was in the way he announced his decision. Instead of listening to Pande, and his principal secretary B.G. Deshmukh, and leaving open the proportion of reservation and other contentious issues to be decided after a national debate, he announced the figure of 27 per cent, and stuck to it till forced by more than a hundred deaths to refer the issue to the Supreme Court in October.

Hindsight also suggests that had he taken the BJP challenge head on, accused it of breaking faith when it announced the decision to support the temple agitation on September 14, and dissolved Parliament he would have come back with his strength enhanced. But he chose to present the people with a fait accompli and fell right into the BJP's trap.

The blame for this lies to a great extent on VP's tendency to seek reassurance from close advisers. This made him vulnerable to sycophants. Two of his ministers, Sharad Yadav and Ram Vilas Paswan, prevailed on him to go for broke on Mandal. As Yadav told a crowd in Patna on October 8, 1990, the "Mandal rath" would crush the "Ram rath". Ironically Yadav and Paswan are now ministers in a BJP-led government.

In the end, however much VP may have erred in the way he implemented Mandal, he will go down in history as a key architect of a new, egalitarian and vibrant India. Far from having started a rebellion that he could not control, he stopped a revolution that would have plunged India into anarchy and threatened its disintegration. What Mandal did was to stop the gap between power and entitlement from widening to the point where those who wielded the former would smash the political system that made possible the latter. That was the democratic Indian state.

Ever since the '60s the middle castes had been accumulating economic power by virtue of the green revolution. But they had been shut out of the power elite because they lacked access to modern, English-based education. This was available only in the cities and therefore by default to an affluent, upper caste, bureaucratic elite. Mandal is giving access to the cities and therefore to the elite to the newly empowered backward classes. What is more it has started a chain reaction in which the Scheduled Castes and Tribes have joined. A grossly iniquitous system of stratification that made some humans inferior to others by birth is breaking down at a dazzling speed. And although a billion people are involved, it is happening almost without violence."

After the ninth Lok Sabha elections in 1989, no political party could get a majority to form the government. Though the Congress Party emerged as a single largest party in the election but it did not stake its claim to form a government. The National Front, which emerged as the second largest party, elected V.P. Singh its leader, and was invited to form the government by the then President R. Venkataraman, with the outside support of the left parties and the BJP. Thus as a result of the 1989 Lok Sabha election, the country witnessed the first minority –cum-coalition government at the Centre, though it was supported by a majority of M.P.'s. As Prime Minister V.P. Singh said his is a minority coalition government with the majority backing of the BJP and CPM.

The V.P. Singh led National Front government remained in power for eleven months and collapsed due to withdrawal of support by the BJP in the wake of the arrest of its leader L.K. Advani during his Rath Yatra. The National Front coalition was destablished only by the power motivations of dissidents (Chandra Shekhar group) in the Janata Dal. It is a classic example of how desperate elements like the congress opposing the coalition governments decision to implement the Mandal Commission's recommendations, the BJP wanted to settle its score on the issue of the Mandir Masjid controversy in Ayodhya raised to sidetrack the Mandal issue and Chandra Shekhar who wanted to avenge the election of V.P. Singh as the leader of Janata Dal in parliament in the wake of his total opposition, had forged on unholy alliance to break up the coalition headed by V.P. Singh. On the working of V.P. Singh's coalition government, President R. Venkataraman observed that his government being dependent on parties with different objectives and ideologies could not withstand pressures from discordant group. The V.P. Singh led government was based on the absolute contradictions, because the CPM, BJP and the Janata Dal were ideologically opposed to one another. The contradictions among the three major political formations were not on marginal issues. They were on the fundamental ideological positions. V.P. Singh as the leader of this political arrangement, who was described as an expert in the art of management of political contradictions, could not sustain it and his government collapsed with in eleven months.

Coalition Government Led By Chandra Shekhar

After the fall of the V.P.Singh led coalition government, the dissent leader Mr. Chandra Shekhar staked his claim to form the government. Congress (I), AIADMK, BJP, Muslim League, National Conference, Kerala Congress and few independent members agreed to support Chandra Shekhar government from outside. It can be said that majority was supporting minority. After the formation of the Chandra Shekhar government, the congress and AIADMK mounted pressure for the dismissal of the DMK government. But the then, Tamil Nadu governor declined to recommend the dismissal of the DMK ministry and therefore he

was

transferred and at last he resigned from the post. Rajiv Gandhi of congress (I) was not satisfied with the Chandra Shekhar government. There was dissatisfaction with government's Gulf Policy, the Punjab initiatives and the deepening economic crisis. However, on the petty issue of surveillance on Rajiv Gandhi, the congress (I) withdrew its support and therefore the ChandraShekhar government resigned. The president R. Venkataraman observed about the working of the Chandra Shekhar led coalition government that he was under constant strain from the pressure of the Congress Party, which assumed that it was a real government and ChandraShekhar only a proxy. "I realized that unequal combinations are always disadvantageous to the weaker side."

Prime Minister ChandraShekhar

Coalition Government led by Deve Gowda

Popular amongst his men and affectionately called as "Mannina Maga" (Son of the soil), Shri H.D.Deve Gowda was born in a farmer family on May 18, 1933 in Hardanahalli villege of Holenarasipura taluk, Hassan District in Karnataka. He secured a Diploma in Civil Engineering from Smt. L V Polytechnic College, Hassan, but preferred to enter into politics. After completing his graduation, he joined Congress Party in 1953 and remained a member till 1962. He became member of State assembly of Karnataka in1962. His political interest was kindled further by his role as President of Anjaneya Cooperative Society and as a member of the Taluk Development Board in a town called Holenarasipura located in Hassan district of Karnataka. His zeal and enthusiasm to work for the people led to his election to the Karnataka State Assembly for six consecutive tenures from 1962 to 1989. He was an independent candidate from Holenarasipura taluk. After the Congress split in 1975, he joined forces with Congress (O) and was elected to the post of Leader of opposition twice between March 1972 and March and March 1976 and once again between November 1976 and December 1977.

Deve Gowda's association with the Janata Dal Party sparked off tenure of resounding success for the Party and Deve Gowda himself. As the President of the Janata Party in 1994, he led the party to a tremendous victory in the state assembly elections. Shri Deve Gowda became Chief Minister of Karnataka.During his term as Chief Minister Deve Gowda reiterated his position as for the poor farmers and brought forward numerous policies, changing lives of farmers and poor.

H. D.Deve Gowda

The 1996 general election once more resulted in a huge parliament. No political party got a clear party verdict from the electorate to form its new government With the three major national combines of BJP, Congress and Janata Dal far short of a simple majority, regional and small parties played a key role in the formation of government at the centre for the first time. In the event, 13 parties apart from the congress support from outside installed Deve Gowda's led coalition government of United Front, after the brief 13 days of the Atal Bihari Vajpayee led BJP government at the Centre.

The United Front Coalition government led by Deve Gowda was like a chariot being pulled at times in different directions by 13 horses. There were personality clashes among the United Front leaders and because of this they lacked cohesion. The ideology had taken a back seat and ego clashes were reigning supreme. As a matter of fact during its existence, the UF steering committee had become a super cabinet and many of the coalition party leaders were trying to act as super Prime Ministers. However the Congress President Sita Ram Kesri's sudden decision to withdraw support from Deve Gowda's Government led to its fall on the floor of the house. No principles, ideologies or welfare programme for the people were involved on either side. Even Deve Gowda's government did not have a view on issue like India should participate in the new international trade regime or whether services such as power and roads should be economically priced. The UF govt. was basically cobbled together with the sole objective of keeping the BJP out of power.

Coalition Government Led by Shri I.K. Gujral

With the fall of the Deve Gowda government, another united front coalition government led by I.K. Gujral assumed power at the centre. Except for the TMC ministers initially the Gowda team itself became the Gujral team. The congress after getting the price of Deve Gowda's head further extended its support to the Gujarat government from outside. However the Gujarat Government also did not last long and in wake of the Jain Commission Report on Rajiv Gandhi's assassination, congress demanded the dropping of DMK members from government and when its demand was not accepted it withdraw support to the government. This led to another midterm poll for the country. Vijay Sanghvi observes that "Prime Minster I.K. Gujarat found himself in a tight position in spite of his intellect and political insight as far as taking any decision on his own is concerned. He in turn was governed by the steering committee of the UF government."

References

1. Chandra, Bipan, et.al. (ed.), *India after Independence1947-2000,* (New Delhi: Penguin Books, 2000) p.259
2. Carras, Mary C., Indira Gandhi –in the Crucible of Leadership, Bombay, 1980, p.100
3. Tariq Ali, the Nehru's and the Gandhi's-An Indian Dynasty, London, 1985, p.194
4. Quoted in Francine R.Frankel, India's Political Economy, 1947-1977, Delhi, 1978, p.576
5. BimalPrasad (ed.), JayaPrakash Narayan, Essential writings (1929-1979), A Centenary Volume (1902-2002), Konark Publishers Pvt.Ltd..Delhi 2002, (p.47)
6. Ibid., p.47
7. Kuldeep Nair, Samved, November 2004, p.145
8. Ibid, p.144
9. Bimal Prasad(ed.), JayaPrakash Narayan, Essential writings(1929-1979),A Centenary Volume(1902-2002),KONARK Publishers Pvt.Ltd..Delhi 2002, (p.48)

10. Dandvate, Madhu, "coalition Politics in India "in Politics India (monthly journal), February 1997, p.24
11. Samved
12. Bipan Chandra, et.al. (ed.), *India after Independence1947-2000,* (New Delhi: Penguin Books, 2000) p.250
13. Ravindra Bharti, Samved, November 2004, p.181
14. Ibid.p.182
15. Shailendra Nath Srivastava, Samved, November 2004, p.31
16. Anchal Sinha, Samved, November 2004, p.162
17. Ashok Bajpai, Samved, November 2004, p.151
18. JayaPrakash Narayan, Prison Diary (Bombay, 1977), pp.132-133

TOTAL REVOLUTION:
JP'S DREAM PROJECT

Jayprakash Narayan, now universally respected and known by the first two initial of his name, J.P., was born on October 11, 1902, in a village Sitab Diara in the Saran District of Bihar, which has now gone to Utter Pradesh due to changing course of the river Saryu. He was from a lower middle class family. His father, Dabu Harshu Dayal, was a Canal officer in the Bihar government. He had some land in his paternal village Sitab Diara, one of whose 'tolas' (localities) is now known as Jayaprakash Nagar.[1]

JP: Early Life

According to Manju Mehta (granddaughter of JP) in his childhood JP's teeth did not develop in his mouth till he became 3 years old. So everyone in his home called him as "Baula" (baby without teeth) and he became "Baula ji". She further recalls that in his childhood whenever he used to go for toilet in night, he used to carry someone with him because he was very scared whenever he went lonely. Again Manju Mehta remembers that Mahatma Gandhi and even Kastoorba came Sitab Diara JP's birth place many times, so feeling of patriotism aroused a very much among its resident and people hear took part in every movement enthusiastically. Everyone including JP's wife Prabhawati burnt Holi (burning something collectively by many people) of foreign goods. People adopted Khadi.[2]

JP received his early education in the local primary school. Later, he passed his Entrance examination from the Patna Collegiate School, winning a Divisional scholarship. He then took admission in Patna College where he studied science and was considered to be a brilliant student. After only one year, he, however, left collage, sought the guidance of Babu Rajendra Prasad (who later became the first President of India) and joined the non-cooperation movement launched by Mahatma Gandhi. After the fires of the first non-cooperation movement had subsided, JP passed the I.Sc examination from the Bihar Vidyapith. He decided, however, not to have his college education controlled by British Government, which had been described by Mahatma Gandhi as a "Satanic Government", and left for America.

JP with few dollars in his pocket, landed in America in October, 1922, to get higher education. He worked as a helper in a fruit shop and a garden and a dishwasher in a hotel for seven long years to earn his keep and to pay for his education. Originally a student of science, after having studied science for three years in an American University, he switched over to arts, to secure a Bachelor's degree. He then studied sociology, especially in Marxian literature and turned a communist. He took his Master of Arts degree in sociology and presented a thesis on "Social Variation" which brought him instant recognition. But that was nothing compared to the heights to which he rose later. He planned to secure a Ph.D. but circumstances forced him to give up the idea and return home.

When he was returning from America, he traveled via London where he met several communist leaders, including RP Dutt. When he came back, he first went to Sabarmati Ashram of Mahatma Gandhi where his wife Prabhwati Devi lived. Gandhi ji treated Prabhawati Devi as his own daughter so JP received the treatment of a son -in –law. In this way JP had easy access to Mahatma Gandhi. Gandhi Ji introduced him to Jawaharlal Nehru. Both Nehru and JP very soon became friends because both held radical views. Nehru invited JP to join The Indian National Congress and participate in freedom movement of India. He also placed JP in charge of the Labour Department of Congress and posted him at its central headquarters at Allahabad. JP was a Marxist and he did not believes in non- violence. But due to his deep love & respect for the Mahatma Gandhi that he joined the freedom movement under his leadership. In the early 30s, when Gandhi ji launched his second non-cooperation movement (the Salt Satyagrah) & all top ranking Congress leaders were arrested & kept behind the bars, JP was made the General Secretary of Indian National Congress and asked to operate from Bombay head quarter of the AICC. Very soon he was recognized as the "brain of the congress". He was arrested in Bombay in 1932 & transferred to Nasik Central Jail, where he came in touch with prominent Marxist like Achyut Patwardhan, Minoo Masani, Purshottam Tricumdes, Ashok Mehta & others. In Nasik prison he got the idea of forming his socialist within the Congress which later came to be known as the Congress Socialist Party (CSP). CSP played a significant role in the country's national & socialist movement. Mahatma Gandhi once referred him as the Master of Indian socialism & declared that "what JP does not know of socialism, no one else in India does". [3]

Though JP joined the congress & movement but he believed in violence. 'So British Government kept a constant watch on his activities & arrested him in 1940 on the charge of opposing British war efforts and kept him in Deoli detention camp in Rajasthan. From the Deoli jail he smuggled out his letter giving detailed instructions to his party men to organize underground revolt against the British government. The letter was intercepted & seized by police men and his plan was disclosed. The British Government published the letter in a distorted form & tried to denigrate him before the people of India. But Mahatma Gandhi immediately came to his rescue. Disassociating from his violent plans,

Mahatma Gandhi condemned the British attempt to malign a patriot like JP. He pleaded for the abolition of the Deoli detention camp. The British govt. abolished the camp and JP was transferred to the Hazaribagh central jail in Bihar.'[4]

When Mahatma Gandhi launched 'Quit India Movement', JP was in prison. Reports of the arrest of Mahatma Gandhi and other leaders made him completely restless. "On the night of November 9th 1942, JP along with three other revolutionaries Yogendra Shukul, Suraj Narayan Singh and Ram Nandon Mishra, managed to scale the 21 feet high walls of the Hazaribagh central jail and escaped."[5]

J.P. as Young Socialist Leader

This news spread like fire in the jungle and it boosted the moral of revolutionaries throughout the country. Though British Government tried hard to suppress the news but every effort went in vein. "JP & his comrades went underground and formed a small army of freedom fighters known as the Azad Dasta. Arrangements were also made to train young recruits in the jungles of the Nepal terai. Some of the top men of Azad Dasta were Archyut Patwardhan, Mrs. Aruna Asif Ali, Dr. Ram Manohar Lohia and Suraj Narayan Singh. Mr. Narayan was its supreme leader. JP also tried to establish on contact with Azad Hind Fauz of Neta ji Subhash Chandra Bose in Burma. The British government launched a man – hunt for JP and his associates and requested the govt. of Nepal to keep an eye on them. JP was arrested by the Nepal police along the other revolutionaries and kept in Hanuman Nagar jail. But before they could be handed over to the Indian police, a column of the Azad Dasta led by Suraj Narayan Singh stormed the jail and after a brief encounter with the guards rescued them."[6]

JP became a legendary figure. "The then Home Minster, Mr. Reginald Maxwell, was after his blood and announced rewards for his arrest. JP was finally arrested on September 18, 1943, while traveling in train to Punjab and was kept in the Lahore Fort. There he was made to lie on ice-slabs and subjected inhuman torture to extract some unworthy confessions from him but he did not bend. He was released on April 11, 1946, only after Mahatma Gandhi had made it a precondition for compromise talks between the Congress and the

British govt."[7]

JP did not like the idea of partitioning of the country. He wished to organize public opinion against the congress scheme of partition but dropped the idea on the advice of Mahatma Gandhi he accepted Mahatma Gandhi's directive against his own will. Later JP regretted this as a blunder on his part. During partition JP and his friends gave their powerful support to Gandhi Ji and Jawaharlal Nehru in controlling the tide of communal frenzy that rocked the Indian sub continent.

Prime Minster Jawaharlal Nehru had once suffered one of the worst indignities of his life in the state capital of Bihar. Nehru could not even address a public meeting at the wheeler Senate Hall in central Patna in the face of an angry and hostile audience. When Nehru failed, JP, who had accompanied him, succeeded in saving the situation and denouncing the angry demonstrator for their scandalous behavior.

Many Biharies living in Calcutta had been the victims of the Calcutta killings in August 1946. Then came the slaughter of Noakholi. But Noakholi had set Bihar ablaze. Frenzied Hindu mobs avenged themselves on defenseless Muslim minorities living in the country side in south Bihar. About 150 members of an armed Hindu mob had been mowed down by police bullets and handgreneds at Nagarnausa (about 40 miles southeast of Patna) and their bodies removed that day to Patna in open trucks. This created tension in the town. When Jawaharlal Nehru went by a car to Senate Hall with JP, he was mobbed as soon as he got down. His jacket was torn, his cap thrown out to the ground and an angry youth tried to throw a garland of shoes on him. Nehru entered the Senate Hall and doors were immediately closed by the Police to prevent further rush of demonstrators. By that time the hall was full mostly with agitated young men who appeared to belong to the Rastriya Swayam Sewak Sangh (RSS). Only two reporters could get inside the hall, one Mr.Narayan Gupta and Mr. S.K. Ghose of the Associated Press of India (which after independence became the Press Trust of India).

As soon as Nehru with JP got up on a table on the built in rostrum of the hall and started addressing the gathering, the angry men greeted him with boos and jeers and refused to listen him. Nehru very soon realized the cause of anger. He in a conciliatory effort said that he was sorry to hear about 100 or 150 Hindus had also been killed in police firing at Nagarnausa. Immediately the audience shouted "Pandrah Sau" (fifteen hundred). The Hall had been surrounded by that time not only by policemen but also British soldiers armed with rifles and stein guns. They were seeing from outside through the glass panes about what was happening inside. At that very moment an electric fuse blew up. The sound could be heard above the din.

The crowed thought that police had opened fire from outside. At once many young men bared their chests and started shouting, "Shoot us Nehru, Shoot us, what else can we expect from you?" Nehru tried his utmost to coax and cajole them to give him a hearing but they refused to listen anything. At this moment demonstration suddenly stopped as JP started bursting with anger at the youths' misconduct, seized the opportunity and started lashing out against the gathering. He accused them that they had disgraced the ancient civilization of India. They had repudiated their religion and traditions by attacking and killing and injuring their weak and helpless neighbors. They had indulged in kidnapping, rape loot and arson. Did their religion teach them to act like beasts? He said that they observed no sympathy and no action taken by the government could be considered harsh enough to quell the communal disturbances and to bring them back to their senses.

The people, who refused to listen Nehru, took JP's address seriously and there was a pin drop silence in the hall.[8]

JP Quit the Congress Party

After independence, JP became increasingly critical of the policies of the congress government. Sardar Patel took very seriously this criticism and he even threatened socialists with disciplinary action. After the assassination of Gandhiji in January, 1948, 'JP, Acharya Narendra Dev and other socialist leaders finally decided to quit the Congress and formed the Socialist Party of India at Nasik. The socialists, who had been returned to the legislatures, resigned. At the Nasik conference of the socialist party JP raised the question of end and means and pleaded for adoption of right means to achieve the noble ends of socialism.'⁹

Although he still called himself a Marxist, he seemed to be moving close to the Gandhian technique and the philosophy of non-violence. He now wanted to change the constitution of the socialist party and term it into a democratic mass organization with open membership as distinguished from restricted membership. A year later in 1949 it was at his instance that the party adopted a new constitution which provided for a mass base with open membership.

Under his leadership the socialist expanded rapidly and soon assumed the shape of a national opposition with promise to become an alternative to the Congress party. The first general election after independence took place in 1952. Elections turned out to be an unequal fight between a well – entrenched and fully financed Congress party on the one side and a disunited opposition on the other side. The socialist had overestimated their strength and contested two thirds of the seats in country. They thus scattered their strength and resources over a much wider area than they could manage. They lost heavily. The election result highlighted the need for consolidation of socialist & democratic masses. 'Due JP's efforts the socialist party & the Krishak Praja Mazdoor Party (KPMP) led by Acharya J.B. Kriplani merged, and the Praja Socialist Party came into being.'¹⁰

When PSP became a political force, Prime Minister Nehru sought its cooperation in the programme of National reconstruction on socialist lines. JP held talks with Nehru at the latter are invitations and submitted a 14 point programme, which Nehru found difficult to implement. This added to the frustration in the socialist rank and file. Some prominent socialist now questioned the correctness of the policy and programme of the party and a bitter ideological conflict followed leading to mutual recriminations.

JP in Bhudan Movement

JP's faith in dialectical materialism had been shaken because he looked for a sound and quick method of achieving socialism through non – violent methods. He had already rejected the violent methods of communism which had failed to create a society based on socialist values in countries where violent revolutions had taken place. At this psychological moment Acharya Vinoba Bhave appeared on the scene with his programme of land distribution through the Bhudan movement. JP felt a great possibility in Bhudan movement of non-violent social change through a change in the general will of the people. JP moved closer to Gandhian philosophy as interpreted by Vinoba Bhave. 'He found in this philosophy a more satisfying answer to the ideological problems of socialism. Ultimately he announced his resolve to become a Jeevandani and dedicate his life to the service of the people at the call of Vinoba Bhave at historic Sarvodaya Conference held at Bodh Gaya in 1954 in the presence of President Rajendra Prasad, Prime Minister Nehru, Acharya Kriplani & other national leaders.'[11]

Vinoba Bhave

It signaled his departure from party politics. Although he continued to be a member of the PSP, his interest in the activities of the party progressively decreased.

Though JP left party progressive, he never failed to raise his voice on national & international issues. He championed the cause of Tibetan independence which was later fully justified by the events. It was only when the Chinese attacked and humiliated India in 1962 that it was universally realized that India's acceptance of Chinese suzerainty over Tibet was a serious blunder. He was the first to take up the cause of Bangladesh. A statement issued by him on March 15, 1971, paying tribute to the heroic people of Bangladesh was repeatedly broad cast by newly freed Dacca Betar Kendra. He helped in establishing a people to people relationship between the India and Bangladesh.

Surrender by Dacoits and Naxalites

One of his historic triumphs of moral persuasion was evident in early 1972 when his "change of heart mission" in Chambal valley brought about the surrender of over 400 notorious dacoits whom all the power of state and police had failed to apprehend & liquidate.[12]

Between 1970 and1972 JP had been devoting his time and energy o eliminating naxlied violence in his Sarvodya way in Musahari block in Muzaffarpur district in north Bihar. In the villages of this block, where the extremists had created a reign of terror with murder & mayhem, the situation return to near normalcy mainly through his efforts.[13]

JP's social service done during the terrible famine of 1967 in Bihar will not be forgotten by the people of the state. He formed the Bihar relief committee and open relieves centers at district, block and panchayat levels and covered practically to two thirds of Bihar & brought succor to the starving people. Despite his falling health, he personally toured the famine stricken areas in the summer heat. But for the tire less efforts of JP, the chairman of the relief committee, many would have died of starvation. The committee continued to function to render relief to the people during flood and drought.

Naga problem and JP

In the case of Nagaland he strongly advocated for a peaceful solution rather than a military solution. At his suggestion Prime Minister Nehru agreed to set up the Nagaland peace mission with JP as one of its members to explore the possibilities of a peaceful settlement. The peace mission was soon able to bring about a ceasefire in Nagaland fallowed by protracted negotiations between representatives of underground Nagas and of the government of India. The Naga question has remained unsolved yet but at least the necessary background was created in which a solution can be found and permanent peace assured. JP's contribution to peace making in Naga land is bearing fruit today.

No lust for power

JP never had a lust for power as he proved it by becoming a Jeevandani although the highest offices in the land were within his reach. Nehru once described JP as the future Prime minister of

India. Whenever the question "after Nehru, who?" was raised, in variably it was JP's name that leapt up. When the question of choosing a successor to President Radha Krishnan arose, all eyes looked up to JP. But JP issued a public statement that president ship should be offered to Dr. Zakir Husain. This would be a proof of India's secularism. Again after the death of Dr. Zakir Husain, national opinion favored for JP for the president ship. Although there was no formal offer, it was known that JP could have become the president if he had so desired. Again he made hi position clear by issuing a statement that he had no desire to be a prisoner in Rashtrapati Bhavan.

Retirement for a short period

JP felt seriously ill at Muzaffarpur only after two days after his 70th birthday then he never recovered his health even partially. At time he had announced his retirement from public activities from October 11, 1972 the purpose of his retirement, according him would be to "read, write & think" more about the future than about the past & present. The challenges to democracy and freedom were upper most in his mind and his thoughts were centering round ways and means to meet them despite his shattering health. He wrote a letter to his associates before his 70th birthday "today, the 11th Oct. 1971, I have completed 69 years of my life. If I live until then, I shall be 70 on Oct.11, 1972. I writing this to tell you of a personal decision that I have taken with the full concurrence of my wife that from Oct.11, 1972, to Oct.11, 1973, i.e. for that entire period of 12 months, I shall withdraw myself completely from any kind of public and social work and sever my connections with every organization with which I am connected now (about 20organization)"[14]

"What I shall do after the expiry of the period of retreat, I do not know. I know only this that until body and mind keep functioning, I shall continue to serve my country and the world. I know after that, the style of my future work will have to change radically because the present style has proved too wasteful of time and energy, both physical and mental. More than this I cannot say at present about my future which really rests in the hands of God."[15]

JP went to his village home in Sitab Diara, where, within a month, he developed a carbuncle in his left hand .he left for Varanasi for medical treatment. There he requested his attending physicians to have a medical checkup of his wife, Mrs. Prabhawati Devi, who had been ailing for the past one year, but had been trying to hide it from him. The results of the medical checkup came as a shock as Prabhawati Devi was suffering from cancer. JP removed her to Bombay without delay. 'The rest he himself needed eluded him completely and the days of his mental agony started and have not ceased even after his wife's death on April 15th, 1973. Through out of his entire married life, Prabhawati, who was issue less, had virtually mothered him. Even at most of his public appearances, she used to be at his side. JP had remained totally dependent on her for almost everything. He deeply loved and respected his wife, without her, he became helpless. Before he then was a big void while his health, never sturdy, started worsening.'[16]

Jayaprakash Narayan and his wife

"JP's attachment to his wife Prabhavathi Devi clearly reflected in his simple act at the railway station. Even as a huge crowd waited eagerly at a distance to welcome him, he did not budge from the place until Prabhavathi Devi joined him after counting all her baggage. He greeted them with Prabhavathi Devi beside him. His gesture touched my heart. "Remembers LAVANAM about this heart touching gesture. He further says, "The couple stayed in a small hut at the Atheist Centre here and I was attending on them. JP's last visit to the city was in the early part of 1975. He was on a nationwide campaign to drum up support against the 'dictatorial policies' of Indira Gandhi. The Sarvodaya members were not in favor of JP's campaign. His tour programme was charted by leaders of Jana Sangh or the R.S.S."[17]

Spousal bond

"But that did not prevent Gora and me from meeting him in the railway station. We were standing aloof, slightly away from the welcome gathering. But JP walked straight to us and asked my father if he had arranged any programme for him. He grew angry when he learnt that our plea to accommodate a small programme at the Atheist Centre was turned down by the organizers of his itinerary.

He called the organizers and told them that the next morning; he would spend two hours at the Atheist Centre from 10 a.m. to 12 noon.

They were surprised and tried to explain to him that they had scheduled other important programmes during the slot. Reacting sharply to their remark, JP said nothing was more important to him in Vijayawada than Gora and his son Lavanam.

We felt completely humbled. At the Atheist, Centre JP spoke for over an hour on the need for democracy above party lines.

It showed that though he was on a mission to mobilize all the opposition parties against Indira Gandhi, his ultimate goal was to achieve democracy above party lines. That was his last visit to the city and his last meeting with Gora.

JP was in jail when Gora died after few months. Soon after his release, he spoke to me on telephone and conveyed his condolences.

Despite adopting a different line of thinking on some issues, what was most striking about JP was his commitment to the cause he had championed for throughout his life."[18]

Meaning of Total Revolution

JP had not given any clear definition of the term Total Revolution. He has expressed his inability to give a comprehensive description of the concept since, according to him; several social variables were in operation. He has, therefore, called upon other social scientists to help him to systematize his ideas about Total Revolution; and he says that, "it will be the fulfillment of one of my dreams if the intellectuals in this country can provide a systematic and comprehensive content to the concept of total revolution."[19]Many writers have tried to understand the term "total revolution.

Revolution in view of JP

JP had been a revolutionary all along and one can see the revolutionary spirit in his thought and action right from his young age. He writes in his Prison Dairy-1975, "I had been bitten by the bug of revolution during my high school days...The revolution bug took me to Marxism and through the national movement to democratic socialism and then to Vinobaji's non-violent revolution through love." In the next paragraph he speaks about his "ancient preoccupation with revolution."[20]

When JP was at school, he and five of his classmates deliberately defied the orders of their headmaster in protest against making the day of Pooja festival a working day. While the other students attended school and wrote the examination fixed for that day these six students boycotted both. During his youth and later on while studying in the America, JP was attracted towards violent revolution and he returned to India in 1929 as a firm believer in it. Moreover, he regarded the entire freedom struggle as a national revolution and stressed the idea of struggle throughout the freedom movement. Hence he was strongly opposed to the parliamentary or constitutional approach, adopted by the congress leadership. Instead he wanted a mass struggle and disapproved of any compromise with the British. Besides, he formed the Congress Socialist Party in order to counteract the parliamentary mentality of the Congressmen and to create 'an instrument of struggle'. Speaking about his personal convictions, he said the following at meeting of Muslims, in 1946: "I was born in a Hindu family, but I call myself a Hindustani and my religion is revolution. I have come here to invite you to join us in the revolution for freedom."[21]

According to JP, every social system becomes outdated and irrelevant in course of time, calling for a change. A new social order needs to be created to suit the demands of time. Hence society brings about constant changes either consciously or unconsciously. But a distinction needs to be made between reactionary changes. The former originate from the under-privileged sections of the society. That is, when there is dissatisfaction among these people a revolutionary situation comes into existence and it derives them to the point of revolt. Hence to JP revolution means first of all a change in the existing social system brought about primarily by the under- privileged class of the society. Such changes are not mere reforms but something more radical than reforms since mere reforms of the structures will not suffice. Only a complete transformation of society and its structures can bring about the desired change. In other words, to JP, while revolution is different from reform, it is identical with transformation.[22]

A revolutionary change is normally very rapid, far-reaching and for reaching and radical. At times it may even lead to a qualitative change in the object. However, JP is not very particular about quick results through his revolutionary movement. He warns Indian people against being tempted by the examples of such revolutions which are carried out through violent means. In 1969, he observed, "my conclusion after a study of violent revolutions is that a violent revolution does bring about a revolution in the sense that it uproots the old social order and destroys it from its foundation. But it fails in achieving the objectives for which the revolution is made."[23]

During the same year he again stressed in course of an article dealing with the theme of revolution that "once the revolutionaries of the day seize power, the people are inescapably subjugated to the juggernaut of the party and the state." Explaining why this happens, he said, "It is not that the violent revolutionaries deceive and betray: it is just the logic of violence working itself out. It cannot be otherwise."[24]

Describing the characteristics of non-violent revolution he observed, "The most important characteristics of this method is that its means must be in harmony with its ends. If the end is a non violent society, the means also must be non-violent; if human freedom is the end, coercive means (except moral coercion) are rule out; if man is an end in himself he cannot be used as a means; if truth is to be the basis of the new life untruthful means are inadmissible; if the end is dispersal of power the means cannot be....Centralized power."[25]

He does not believe in a sudden change, but in a gradual process. So he said on June 22nd, 1974 that "one step at a time is enough for me".[26]

He expressed same idea in his prison diary - 1975, "the revolution being peaceful, it was not to happen suddenly and swiftly. It would take time, but the times being revolutionary, not too much time – perhaps a space of a decayed or two."[27]

According to JP another essential characteristic of a revolution is struggle. This struggle is in a way dialectical –between individual and society, authority and freedom, the elite and the masses, property and non possession, labor and capital. This atmosphere of struggle cannot be created at will. The need and the conditions for the struggle have to evolve through a historic process. Both "social and historical condition have to be ripe before a revolution can succeed. Therefore, the revolutionary struggle cannot take place until a given society is ready for it inwardly. But once it is ready, it will begin to act and no one can stop it. The struggle will lead to a successful end; a revolution will have taken place. This atmosphere will be present when the general public, particularly the youth and the intelligentsia, experience wide spread disaffection, frustration, disillusionment and alienation from authority. These are caused by the suppression of the aspirations of the human spirit for freedom, joy and self realization.[28]

For JP revolution means not only struggle but also construction. He says that "this double process of struggle and construction is essential if there is to be a complete revolution. When both struggle & construction take place there is hope for the creation a new social order. A revolution for his creation of a new social order can never be preplanned. It erupts spontaneously, like a volcano. JP says that no revolution can in history has taken place "according to a preconceived pattern laid down in a text book, be that the book of Marx, of Lenin, of Mao or of anybody else. Every revolution writes its own text book..."[29]such spontaneity is another characteristic of a revolution.

Meaning of Total for JP

Although the concept of total revolution took definite shape during the final phase of JP's political philosophy the idea it did exist in his mind much earlier. On several occasions in the earlier phases of his political thoughts process he has talked, directly or indirectly, about total revolution. Like as early as 1942 he used an expression very similar to total revolution. In his first letter to the freedom fighter, entitled "To all fighters of freedom" and written in1942, JP spoke about the need for a "total revolt" of the masses as the objective of the struggle. By this expression he meant an all out revolt, in every way, to attain national independence. Thus though JP meant by "total revolt" something different from what he would mean by total revolution later, the similarity of the two expressions is worth noting. According to Sachidanand, JP used the expression 'total revolution' in 1946 in a message to a certain professor, Yamuna Verma. However, Sachidanand admits that at that time JP's ideas about 'total revolution' had not developed much.

JP used more directly this expression in his article "A picture of Sarvodaya social order", written in the mid 50s. Talking about Bhudan Movement in that article he said that it was "the first step towards a total revolution- social, political & economic. In his "Letter to PSP Members" written in 1957, JP talked about Total Revolution indirectly at least twice. In one place he spoke of a 'total agrarian revolution'. Later, he spoke about a moral, economic, political & social revolution through *gramdan movement*.

By the word total JP means "a revolution in all aspects of the life of the society and the individual. He was not asking for a mere change of a particular govt. or changes only in the political sphere. He wants a change in every aspects of society he says while talking about the Bihar Movement, that "it should encompass the totality of human relation and social organizations". It is in this sense of comprehensiveness that he identifies 'Total' with social revolution, in his prison diary where he speaks of 'social or total revolution. JP did not make any distinction between the words total and whole, though he is aware that these two words are not synonymous. Yet for the purpose of his concept of total revolution he uses these two words interchangeably. Therefore, total means whole, affecting each sphere entirely or completely. It indicates the intensity of the revolution. It wants to transform every sphere not just superficially or partially but entirely.

The idea of total has a communitarian aspect too. JP's revolution has its starting point at the grassroots level where the masses are involved;

entire community has to carry on the struggle for total revolution. It is a communitarian revolution.

Total revolution as a whole

When he assembled these various elements of the meaning of revolution and enumerated and explained earlier, we get a definition of total revolution. Comprehensiveness, completeness and communitarians are the basic element of total. JP has conceived of revolution as a radical change brought about by the people through continuous struggle and constructive work. Thus Total revolution can be described as a comprehensive and complete change brought about by the active participation of the entire community through a long process of peaceful struggle and constructive work. JP is not at all dogmatic about the meaning of total revolution. He says that "at different times a total revolution might take different meanings in the sense that its contents might also be different." The definition and application of this concept thus will be conditioned by time and the prevailing situation. To that extent the meaning of the concept remains relative and flexible. Hence he said that the Bihar movement was writing its own text book. JP is not confining himself to any rigid ideology or ism. In an attempt to explain further the meaning of total revolution, JP divides the scope of the concept into seven ideological spheres, namely, political, economic, social, cultural, education, ideological or intellectual and spiritual.

When asked to explain what he meant by social, economic and cultural revolution, JP replied "I have just tried to show that in the word 'total' I included all these? But there may be other aspects of individual and social life which I have forgotten to mention. That also would be affected by a total revolutionary movement. Hence the division into different sphere is not essential. What is important is the fact that every aspect of man's life is included in the concept and that each of these spheres will have to undergo for reaching changes.

Many people think that JP had for the first time used the term "total revolution" but actually it was Karl Marx who had first used this term more than a century & a quarter before JP popularized it. Writing in the poverty of philosophy (1847), he remarks "Mean while the antagonism between the proletariat & the bourgeoisie is a struggle of class again class, a struggle which carried to its highest expression is a total revolution." In a different sense, i.e. signifying a radical transformation not merely of our material conditions but also of the moral character of the individual the idea total revolution was implicit in many of Gandhi's writings & speeches. Vinoba Bhave further expanded the idea, according to him "my aim is to bring about a threefold revolution. First, I want a change in people's heart; secondly, I want to create a change in their lives; and thirdly, I want to change the social structure." In the 60s he spoke in this vein frequently enough to warrant the use of 'towards total revolution' as the title of a book containing his speeches, published in 1968. At least once he also used the term total revolution. It has been aptly observed in a recent study that JP's movement for total revolution was a continuation of the preceding movement for non-violent revolution through Bhodan and Gramdan. JP was fully justified in remarking on one occasion: "there is hardly any difference between Sarvodaya and total revolution. If there is any, then Sarvodaya is the goal and total revolution the means. Total revolution is basic change in all aspects of life. There cannot be Sarvodaya without this." JP Referring to the Bhodan and Gramdan programmes observed, "Gandhi's non-violence was not just a plea for law & order, or a cover for status quo, but a revolutionary philosophy. It is needed a philosophy of total revolution, because it embraces personal and social ethics and values of life as much as economic, political and social institutions and processes." However, it is a fact that the term 'Total Revolution' became a recurrent theme of JP's speeches and writings only since 1974 and it is only since then that it has taken its place in Indian political discourse.

Total Revolution Defined By Others

Some other writers and thinkers have tried to understand and define the meaning of the term total revolution. Like Nageshwar Prasad thinks that moral values receive primary emphasis in the concept of total revolution. K.B.Y. Thottappa understands the concept as "a mental & moral revolution, first and last in the individual man, which would as such be writ large in society as well." A radical change in the mental outlook & a spiritual regeneration of the individual members are envisaged here. Such a change will in turn give birth to a new time of relationship among the members of a particular community, thus ensuring the integration of the individual & the community.

Another element which has been emphasized by writers is the eradication of the existing evils. Like N.G. Goray said that "JP's concept of total revolution is synonymous with the concept of total emancipation of man." It means that, through total revolution JP wants to eradicate all the evils of social life & liberate man from their impact & influences. Similarly A. Appadorai too emphasized that total revolution is "an all-comprehensive social revolution including elimination of corruption, unemployment, untouchably & out-molded social customs like dowry & so on. V.M. Tarkunde, V.B. Karnik and Sachinanda Nand underline the role of the people. According to Tarkunde, the concept of total revolution relies primarily on people's power, created through a cultural resurgence. Karnik points out how the concept of total revolution emphasizes the need for the participation of the entire population without excluding any section. Sachidanand said "by revolution JP meant basic change in the power structure, both political and economic and by total revolution he meant the transfer of total power to the people. The transfer of total power to the people clearly means a genuine democracy and the decentralization of power. Indian Express (Delhi) brings out this point. It views the meaning total revolution basically as struggle for 'the restoration of those values by which our democracy can be made more representative and more responsive.' This implies the editorial of Indian Express goes on to say, 'the rebuilding of our social & political structure from the ground up.' Prabhu Das Patwari says that to JP total revolution meant a revolution 'from the village upwards to the largest urban concentration, by forming people's committees at all levels. These will usher in *lokniti* (rule by the people) in the place of *rajniti* (rule by the state) and generate people's power that will control state power.' Nageshwar Prasad also stresses at this point, according to him, the decentralization of authority is one of the chief elements of the concept of total revolution.

All these writers focused at total revolution have to be brought about only through non-violence means. These writers have brought out several elements of the concept of total revolution: it is a process and a continuous struggle, it is based primarily on moral principles, it stresses internal as well as external transformation. It makes people's participation essential, it aims at a genuine democracy with a decentralized power structure, it calls for radical changes in the existing structures. It seeks to eradicate all social evils, and finally it hopes to achieve all these through non-violence.

JP's ideas on India's foreign policy

JP's vision was not confined to India, but encompassed the whole world. He keenly looked forward to India devoting herself to the cause of freedom and peace all over the world. While generally supporting the policy of non-alignment and proud and happy that India was doing her best for the causes of freedom and peace all over the world, whenever he felt that India's foreign policy was deviating from the path, he came out with a strong criticism of that policy, working as the nation's sentinel in this as in other fields. Sometimes his stand on certain foreign policy issue made him quite unpopular with the Indian elite, but that failed to deflect him from advocating the line he had taken up, provided he continued to consider it as conductive to the causes of freedom and peace in the world as well as to India's own interests

His second letter to fighters of freedom, issued in September 1943, while he was working underground after his escape from Hazaribagh central prison, gives us a glimpse of his vision on India's role in world affairs even before the achievement of independence. At a time when a section of Indian nationalist leadership(represented by Jawaharlal Nehru) felt inclined towards the united nations led by the USA, Britain, U.S.S.R., and china, and the other (represented by Subhash Chandra Bose) towards the Axis powers led by Germany & Japan. JP adopted a third line. Inclining neither to the one nor the other of the two groupings of world powers he asserted that the future lay not with either of the two power blocs, but with the common people all over the world and India should do its best to bring them together for strengthening the forces of freedom and peace. This idea contain the germ of the concept of a third force in world affairs, forcefully articulated later by Ram Manohar Lohia and forming the basic of the foreign policy outlook of the socialist party after the achievement of independence.

JP generally supported non-alignment, but strongly felt that sometimes its implementation by Nehru was not satisfactory and indeed resulted in its distortion, making it, in effect, a shield for weakness that encouraged aggression. Such criticism was related particularly to India's policy towards Soviet suppression of the nationalist uprisings in Hungary (1956) and Czechoslovakia (1968) and similar Chinese action in Tibet (1959). In the case of Hungary, there is no doubt that Nehru's sympathy were with its people and he publicly acknowledged that their uprising against Soviet domination in 1956 represented their national upsurge, he did not express such a view immediately on hearing about that uprising. Even later he was extremely cautious in the choice of words and to care to ensure that they did not in any way offend the Soviet union, who support India badly needed in order to deal with the problem created by the US military alliance with Pakistan. JP was not convinced such reasoning and was shocked beyond measure by Nehru's attitude. He was more aghast with the performance of V.K. Krishna Menon, then India's representative in the UN, who declared in course of the debate on the Hungarian question in the General Assembly that that was a domestic affair of the Hungarian people and refused to condemn the Soviet action there. JP reacted strongly, "as an Indian, I hang down my head in shame that a spokes man of my country should have gone so far in cynical disregard of the truth and the fundamental principles of freedom and peace that are said to guide our international conduct."

JP was also forthright in his criticism of Soviet Union on the occasion of its military intervention in Czechoslovakia in order to suppress the upsurge of liberalism in 1968 under the leadership of Dubchek. In a statement issued to the press on 22nd August 1968, he remarked "this is an occasion for deep mourning and fervent prayer. Once again might has triumphed over right and the law of jungle prevailed. Russia has violated everything descent in human civilization." JP adopted a similar attitude towards the Tibetan uprising in 1959. As the president of the All India Tibet Convention he convened an Afro-Asian Convention on Tibet in New Delhi in April 1960 to draw the world's attention to the Tibetan issue. In course of his presidential address to it he declared that Tibet had been an independent country before it was annexed by China and, like other countries of the world, it too was entitled to remain free and retain its rights of self-determination.

JP was equally critical of the US whenever he found that it was following in imperialistic policy. Thus in 1050 when the US announced its decision to defend Formosa, where the leaders of the Kuomintang Government had taken shelter and to support the continuation of that government's representation in the UN on the seat earmarked for China. JP issued a strong statement denouncing American decision, "It is pity that the successors of the great tradition of Roosevelt are acting as the swaggering imperialists of an age that has ended forever." He further added, "The peoples of India Asia desire and need the friendship of such world powers as America and Russia, but they are awakened enough now to spurn any gesture of domination." JP adopted a similar attitude towards the continued occupation of South Vietnam by the US in the 60s. Referring to the war in Vietnam as 'an issue of the gravest significance', he strongly debunked the US claim to be fighting the battle of freedom and democracy there and asserted that if the people anywhere wished freely to choose communism, no one had the right to forcibly prevent them from doing so.

JP in the case of Nepal was deeply interested in the struggle for democracy there, which gathered momentum after the achievement of India's independence from British rule in1947. Some of the prominent leaders of that movement particularly B.P. Koirala, were among his close personal friends. JP and his party were actively helping that struggle which was being carried on from its base in India. When Prime Minister Nehru expressed his unease at this and reminded JP that Nepal, although a part of the Indian subcontinent, was an independent country and it might not be proper for a struggle against the then existing government in that country to be allowed to be conducted from Indian soil, the latter sharply differed from that view. He pointed out in his reply that India as a free, democratic country must performed its due role in the promotion of freedom and peace in the world at large by working as a safe heaven for all those who were fighting against tyranny and oppression in their own countries. That, he asserted, would be in accord the policies of Britain and other democratic countries in Western Europe.

Regarding National freedom Movements anywhere in the world JP showed sympathy for masses who were struggling for peace and freedom in their respective mother land. JP said "I have been a fighter for freedom all my life and for me National frontiers are of no significance. If freedom is in peril anywhere I, as a humble citizen of the world, reserve to myself the right to raise my voice. India and Nepal are close neighbors and I cannot shut my eyes to what is happening there simply because Nepal is separate country.

JP was keenly interested in establishment of friendly relation between India and Pakistan. Although he strongly opposed the partition India but once partition became a reality he always pleaded for adoption of a friendly attitude towards Pakistan so that the ill effects of partition might be removed and the two countries lived in peace and harmony. He recognized the difficulties in the way, but was convinced that if a positive approach was adopted by the leaders of both the countries and serious efforts were made to create an atmosphere of trust between them, it was not impossible to settle all the disputes between them step by step and lay the foundations for a harmonious relationship. With this purpose in view he founded in 1962 an organization named India –Pakistan conciliation Group with himself as chairman and close friend, J.J. Singh, as secretary. This group worked seriously for improving India Pakistan relation. In 1964, JP led a good will delegation to Pakistan on its behalf and met a no. of leaders there to promote cooperation between the two countries. His perspective on India Pakistan relation comes out clearly in the following extract from one of his speeches in 1964 "relations between India and Pakistan are on an entirely different footing from those between other countries. India and Pakistan are two different countries, two different states, but they are the home of one single people. I do not think that this basic truth has been fully appreciated either by the Indians or Pakistanis. Let me say at outset that partition, as the 17years of post independence history of India and Pakistan have conclusively proved, has been a complete failure .it has solved no problem, but has created many more than existed before. Yet partition is a fact and has to be accepted. But the ill effects of the partition must be removed. They can be removed not by force, not by coercion, not by conquest. They can be removed only by love, by understanding, by cooperation."

In the case of Bangladesh he immediately understood the significance of the upsurge in Bangladesh under the leadership of Sheikh Mujibur Rahman. As early as March 16, 1971 he issued a statement to the press expressing his deep admiration for Mujib's leadership, particularly his extraordinary success in uniting his people behind him and his forbearance and wisdom in the face much provocation. He, however, made it clear that his statement was not prompted by any anti - Pakistani motivation. Just as he believe in the territorial integrity of his own country, he said, he did not wish to see the breakup of Pakistan and hoped that those in power in west Pakistan would act wisely and concede the demand for autonomy voiced by the people of Bangladesh. When this hope did not materialized and the rulers of Pakistan ordered a military crackdown, JP came out with another statement on 27, March, declaring that what was happening in Pakistan was surely not that countries not internal matter alone and that India was deeply concerned with it. While recognizing the delicate position in which the government of India was placed, he wanted a to at least try to ensure that no country gave any armed assistance to the military dictatorship in Pakistan nor any facilities to enable her armed forces and supplies to be moved from the west to the east. As news of the ruthless suppression of the freedom fighters in Bangladesh poured in, JP was stirred to further activity. On 2nd April he came out with his third press statement on the struggle in Bangladesh and declared that Indian people must move beyond resolutions and expressions of sympathy and do all that might be required to ensure that the armed might of west Pakistan was not able to crush that struggle "all help required for this purpose must be made available without any further delay." While the nature of the assistance might be left to the government to decide, JP affirmed that his sense of history and knowledge of international affairs told him that it would not be any violation of international law to accord immediate recognition to Bangladesh. He was one of the earliest voices in this regard.

JP convinced an international conference on Bangladesh in New Delhi in the third week of Sep. 1971 with the twin purpose of influencing world public opinion and galvanizing India into effective action for the liberation of Bangladesh. It was attended by nonoofficial representatives from 25 countries, including among them parliamentarians, jurists, retired ministers and diplomats' journalist and other molders of public opinion. In his presidential address JP observed " you know how vitally that situation affects India, not only on account of the presence of 8.5 million refugees, whose nos. are daily mounting up, but also because instability and social tensions in the whole eastern region of India thwart normal administration and development programmes in the area, and enable Pakistan to achieve a demographic redistribution of its population at the cost of India... most important of all, the situation in Bangladesh is a continuing threat to security of India and the peace the subcontinent, perhaps of the whole of south Asia." When no action on the part of India was taken he became more & more insistent on such action. He openly said in a article published in a New Delhi paper "having failed in all our diplomatic efforts, we should now take courage in both our hands, accord formal recognition even at this late hour to the Bangladesh government headed by Sheikh Mujibur Rahman and then go all out to help them to win their independence. That might precipitate a war with Pakistan, but it is a contingency for which we have to be prepared in any case." JP was indeed so impatient for action that he went on to declared that Indira Gandhi was "throwing dust into the eyes of the people of this country" by asserting that all possible help could be given to the freedom struggle in Bangladesh even without recognizing its government.

JP recalling that it had been the dream of some Indian leaders including Nehru, Lohia, Vinoba Bhave and himself, that "the destiny not only of the Indian sub continent but also of the entire south Asia region lies in some kind of association or community of the nations of the region," he observed in curse of a letter to Sheikh Mujibur Rahman on 31st January 1972 "my reason for sharing this dream with you is because I feel that you have the moral & political stature , the breadth of vision and largeness of heart & the unique position in the whole of south Asia , as well as the practical attitude of mind....that are necessary for such an imaginative , constructive and reconciliatory task . Besides, at 51 you have all the time needed to meet such a challenging historic task."

Dr. Ram Manohar Lohia

Ram Manohar Lohia was born on March 23, 1910 in a village named Akbarpur in the District of Faizabad. Ram's father, Hira Lal, was a nationalist by spirit and a teacher by profession. His mother, Chanda, died when Ram was very young. Ram was introduced to the Indian freedom struggle at an early age by his father through the various protest assemblies Hira Lal took his son to. Ram made his first contribution to the freedom struggle by organizing a small hartal on the death of Lokmanya Tilak.

Hira Lal, an ardent follower of Gandhiji, took his son along on a meeting with the Mahatma. This meeting deeply influenced Lohia and sustained him during trying circumstances and helped seed his thoughts, actions and love for swaraj. Ram was so impressed by Gandhiji's spiritual power and radiant self-control that he pledged to follow the Mahatma's footsteps. He proved his allegiance to Gandhiji, and more importantly to the movement as a whole, by joining a Satyagraha march at the age of ten!

While in school reading the prescribed history book, Lohia noted that the British author of the textbook referred to the great Maharashtrian king Chatrapati Maharaja Shivaji as a "bandit leader" (lutera sardar). Lohia researched the facts and proved that the label "bandit leader" was an unjust description of the Maharaja. Lohia launched a campaign to have the description stricken from the textbook. Lohia organized a student protest in 1918 to protest the all-white Simon Commission which was to consider the possibility of granting India dominion status without requiring consultation of the Indian people.

Lohia met Jawaharlal Nehru in 1921. Over the years they developed a close friendship Lohia, however, never hesitated to censure Nehru on his political beliefs and openly expressed disagreement with Nehru on many key issues.

Lohia attended the Banaras Hindu University to complete his intermediate course work after standing first in his school's metric examinations. In 1929, Lohia completed his B.A. from Calcutta University. He decided to attend Berlin University, Germany over all prestigious educational institutes in Britain to convey his dim view of British philosophy. He soon learned German and received financial assistance based on his outstanding academic performance.

While in Europe, Lohia attended the League of Nations assembly in Geneva. India was represented by the Maharaja of Bikaner, a well known puppet of the British Raj. Lohia took exception to this and launched a protest there and there from the visitors' gallery. He fired several letters to editors of newspapers and magazines to clarify the reasons for his protest. The whole incident made Lohia a recognized figure in India overnight. Lohia helped organize the Association of European Indians and became secretary of the club. The main focus of the organization was to preserve and expand Indian nationalism outside o Lohia wrote his PhD thesis paper on the topic of "Salt Satyagraha," focusing on Gandhiji's socio-economic theory.

Lohia as a student

When Lohia returned to India in 1933, a comical situation arouses. Ram had no money to reach his hometown from the airport. He quickly wrote a nationalistic article for "The Hindu," the most popular and widely read newspaper and got money to pay for the fare home.

Lohia joined the Indian National Congress as soon as he returned home. Lohia was attracted to socialism and helped lay the foundation of Congress Socialist Party, founded 1934, by writing many impressive articles on the feasibility of a socialist India. Lohia formed a new branch in the Indian National Congress--the All India Congress Committee (a foreign affairs department). Nehru appointed Lohia as the first secretary of the committee. During the two years that he served he helped define what would be India's foreign policy.

In the onset of the Second World War Lohia saw an opportunity to collapse the British Raj in India. He made a series of caustic speeches urging Indians to boycott all government institutions. He was arrested on May 24, 1939, but released by authorities the very next day in fear of a youth uprising.

Soon after his release, Lohia wrote an article called "Satyagraha Now" in Gandhiji's newspaper, Harijan on June 1, 1940. Within six days of the publication of the article, he was arrested and sentenced to two years of jail. During his sentencing the Magistrate said, "He (Lohia) is a top-class scholar, civilized gentleman, and has liberal ideology and high moral character." In a meeting of Congress Committee Gandhiji said, "I cannot sit quiet as long as Dr. Ram Manohar Lohia is in prison. I do not yet know a person braver and simpler than him. He never propagated violence. Whatever he has done has increased his esteem and his honor." Lohia was mentally tortured and interrogated by his jailers. On December of 1941, all the arrested Congress leaders, including Lohia, were released in a desperate attempt by the government to stabilize India internally.

Gandhiji and the Indian National Congress launched the Quit India movement in the 1942. Prominent leaders, including Gandhiji, Nehru, Azad and Patel, were jailed. The "secondary cadre" stepped-up to the challenge to continue the struggle and to keep the flame for swaraj burning within the people's hearts. Leaders who were still free carried out their operations from underground. Lohia printed and distributed many posters, pamphlets and bulletins on the theme of "Do or Die," on his secret printing-press. Lohia along with freedom fighter Usha Mehta, broadcast messages in Bombay for three whole months before detection from a secret radio station called "Congress Radio" as a measure to give the disarrayed Indian population a sense of hope and spirit in absence of their leaders.

Lohia went to Calcutta to revive the movement there. He changed his name to hide from the police who were closing in on him. Lohia fled to Nepal's dense jungles to evade the British. There he met the Nepalese people and Koirala brothers (courageous freedom fighters in Nepal), who remained Lohia's allies rest of their lives.

Lohia was captured in May of 1944, in Bombay. Lohia was taken to a prison in Lahore, notoriously known throughout India for its tormenting environment. In the prison he underwent extreme torture. His health was destroyed but his courage remained. Even though he was not as fit his courage and willpower strengthened through the ordeal. Under Gandhiji's pressure the Government released Lohia and his comrade Jayaprakash Narayan. A huge crowd waited to give the 2 a hero's welcome. Lohia decided to visit his friend in Goa to relax. Lohia was alarmed to learn that the Portuguese government had censured the people's freedom of speech and assembly. He decided to deliver a speech to oppose the policy but was arrested even before he could reach the meeting location. The Portuguese government relented and allowed the people the right to assemble. The Goan people weaved Lohia's tale of unselfish work for Goa in their folk songs. As India's tryst with freedom neared Hindu-Muslim strife increased. Lohia strongly opposed partitioning India in his speeches and writings. He appealed to communities in riot torn regions to stay united, ignore the violence surrounding them and stick to Gandhiji's ideals of non-violence. Lohia comforted the Mahatmas as nation that once wielded the power of non-violence took refuge in killing their own brothers and sisters. Lohia remained beside Gandhiji as son would remain beside a father.

Dr. Lohia was the first to introduce the unification of some 650 Indian princely states together to form larger states, an idea later adopted by Sardar Patel, first Home Minister of India. Lohia favored Hindi as the official language of India, arguing, "The use of English is a hindrance to original thinking, progenitor of inferiority feelings and a gap between the educated and uneducated public. Come; let us unite to restore Hindi to its original glory."

He was one of the greatest thinkers the Indian Parliament would ever see. He realized that the prevailing poverty would create an India with a weak foundation. As an economically crippled country India tried to find ways to get rid of its abject poverty, Lohia decided to make the mass public realize the importance of economic robustness for the nation's future.

A brilliant intellectual, a Ph.D. from Berlin (1932), fluent in English, German, French, Hindi and Bengali, he routinely fought battles on behalf of India's poorest, speaking out about injustice and poverty sharply and without let-up. When he arrived in Parliament in 1963, the country had had a one-party government through three general elections. Lohia shook things up. He had written a pamphlet, "25000 Rupees a Day", the amount spent on Prime Minister Jawaharlal Nehru, an obscene sum in a country where the vast majority lived on 3 annas (less than one-quarter of a rupee) a day. Nehru demurred, saying that India's Planning Commission statistics showed that the daily average income was more like 15 annas (a little under a rupee) per day. Lohia demanded that this was an important issue, one that cried out for a special debate. The controversy, still remembered in India as the "Teen Anna Pandrah Anna (3 annas -15 annas)" controversy, saw something akin to the tense excitement of "Mr. Smith Goes to Washington". Member after member gave up his time to Lohia as he built his case, demolishing the Planning Commission statistics as fanciful. Not that the Commission was attempting to mislead, but the reality was that a small number of rich people were pulling up the average to present a wholly unrealistic picture. At that time, Lohia's figure was true for over 70% of the population.

Unlike the Marxist theories which became fashionable in the third world in the 50's and 60's, Lohia recognized that caste, more than class, was the huge stumbling block to India's progress. Then as today, caste was politically incorrect to mention in public, but most people practiced it in all aspects of life - birth, marriage, association and death. It was Lohia's thesis that India had suffered reverses throughout her history because people had viewed themselves as members of a caste rather than citizens of a country. Caste, as Lohia put it, was congealed class.

Class was mobile caste. As such, the country was deprived of fresh ideas, because of the narrowness and stultification of thought at the top, which was comprised mainly of the upper castes, Brahmins and Baniyas, and tight compartmentalization even there, the former dominant in the intellectual arena and the latter in the business. A proponent of affirmative action, he compared it to turning the earth to foster a better crop, urging the upper castes, as he put it, "to voluntarily serve as the soil for lower castes to flourish and grow", so that the country would profit from a broader spectrum of talent and ideas.

He encouraged public involvement in post-freedom reconstruction. He pressed people to construct canals, wells and roads voluntarily in their neighborhood. He volunteered himself to build a dam on river Paniyari which is standing till this day and is called "Lohia Sagar Dam." Lohia said, "satyagraha without constructive work is like a sentence without a verb." He felt that public work would bring unity and a sense of awareness in the community. He also was instrumental in having 60 percent of the seats in the legislature reserved for minorities, lower classes, and women.

As a democracy, the Indian Parliament was obliged to listen to citizens' complaints. Lohia helped create a day called "Janavani Day" on which people from around the nation would come and present their grievances to Members of Parliament. The tradition continues even today.

Lohia wanted to abolish private schools and establish upgraded municipal (government) schools which would give equal academic opportunity to students of all casts. This he hoped would help eradicate the divisions created by the caste system.

At the Socialist Party's Annual Convention, Lohia set up a plan to decentralize the government's power so that the general public would have more power in Indian politics. He also formed Hind Kisan Panchayat to resolve farmers' everyday problems.

Lohia was a socialist and wanted to unite all the socialists in the world to form a potent platform. He was the General Secretary of Praja Socialist Party. He established the World Development Council and eventually the World Government to maintain peace in the world.

During his last few years, besides politics, he spent hours talking to thousands of young-adults on topics ranging from Indian literature, politics and art.

Lohia died on October 12, 1967 in New Delhi. He left behind no property or bank balance but prudent contemplations.

Rajnarayan

Rajnarayan was an Indian politician who contested Lok Sabha election against Prime Minister Indira Gandhi from RaiBareli constituency. He defeated Mrs. Gandhi in this election and became well known figure in Indian politics and history thereafter. He was earlier defeated by her in the Lok Sabha elections of 1971.

Rajnarayan accused India Gandhi of corrupt electoral practices and filed a petition in Allahabad High Court against her. The court on June, 12th 1975 in its decision upheld the accusations and set aside election of India Gandhi. The court disqualified her to contest Lok Sabha elections of six years.

Rajnarayan was born in 1917 in a village named Motikoat, Gangapur in Varanasi district of Uttar Pradesh. He was from the royal family of Varanasi and directly associated with Maharaja Chet Singh and Maharaja Balwant Singh, who were kings of Varanasi, over a century back. He obtained degrees of MA and LLB.

He joined socialist party and held many positions. He was very close to Dr. Ram Manohar Lohia. Dr. Lohia described him as "a person who has heart of a Lion and practices of Gandhi". Dr.

Lohia admired him a lot and even said that "if in India there could be just three or four persons like him, dictatorship can never shadow the democracy". He was elected to Uttar Pradesh Legislative Assembly in 1952. He became first leader of opposition in the Assembly after independence, and his second term ended in 1962. He was member of Rajya Sabha, the upper house of Indian Parliament from 1966 to 1972 and again from 1974 to 1976. He became Union Minister of Health in Morarji Desai Government from 1977 to 1980. He is one of the strongest pillars of socialist movement in India along with Dr. Ram Manohar Lohia.

Rajnarayan

He was a great freedom fighter. He was president of student congress during 1942 revolution, and he led the revolution in and around Varanasi district. The protest and revolution under his leader ship is considered as one of the best this country has ever seen on august 09, 1942. He was so active in freedom struggle that British government wanted to get a hold of him and ordered to prize anybody who can get him "dead or alive". The prize for getting him dead or alive was Rs. 5000, in the year 1942.

Lohia is often called a maverick socialist, a clichéd but nevertheless apt description. But he gave that impression not to be controversial, but because he was always evolving his thoughts, and like his mentor, Gandhi, did not hesitate to speak the truth as he saw it. He often surprised both supporters and opponents. He astounded everyone by calling for India to produce the bomb, after the Chinese aggression of 1962. He was anti-English, saying that the British ruled India with bullet and language (*bandhook ki goli aur angrezi ki boli*). Full of unforgettable phrases which would characterize a point of view, he captured who was a member of India's ruling class in with near-mathematical precision that I have not seen bettered in three decades -- "high-caste, wealth, and knowledge of English are the three requisites, with anyone possessing two of these belonging to the ruling class". The definition still holds.

Ram Manohar Lohia was regarded by friend and foe alike as an honest, brilliant, and profound man. He inspired deep loyalty and enormous respect, and to his followers, the words "Doctor Sahib" would conjure up only one image. He lived and died in simplicity, owning nothing. His death was a huge loss to India, for she had lost her one of her finest political minds. He was only 57.

He holds a record for going jail eighty times in his total life span of 69 years. He spent nearly 17 years in jail for the greater cause of society and country. He passed away on December 31, 1986 in a hospital at Delhi which was later named after him as Dr. Ram Manohar Lohia Hospital.

References

1. S.K.Ghosh, The crusade and the End of Indira Raj, (New Delhi: Intellectual book Centre, 1978), p.14
2. Manju Mehta, India News May 26-June 1, 2007
3. S.K.Ghosh, The crusade and the End of Indira Raj,(New Delhi: Intellectual book Centre, 1978), p.15
4. Ibid, p.16
5. Ibid
6. Ibid, pp.16-17
7. Ibid, p.17
8. Ibid, p.18-19
9. Ibid, p.21

10. Ibid, p.22

11. Ibid, pp.22-23s

12. Ibid, p, 24

13. Ibid

14. Ibid, p.25

15. Ibid

16. Ibid, p.26

17. The Hindu,2 September 2006

18. Ibid

19. JP, "Forword"to J.D.Sethi, Gandhi Today,Vikas Publising house,New Delhi,1978,p.11

20. JP, Prison Diary -1975, p.25 (August 21)

21. Quoted in M.Bharthan, Jayaprakash Narayan: A study in Sarvodaya, unpublished Doctoral Thesis, University Of Madras, 1976, p.36

22. JP, "Towards Total Revolution-1: Search for an Ideology",Popular Prakashan,Bombay,1978 , p.93

23. Bimal Prasad, (ed.), A Revolutionary's Quest: Selected Writings Of Jaya Prakash Narayan (New Delhi, 1980), pp.285-286

24. Ibid., p.290

25. Ibid., p.294

26. Ibid., p.295

27. Quoted in The Hindustan Times, June 23, 1974

28. JP, Prison Diary -1975, p.21 (August 18)

29. JP, *"Dynamics of Real Revolution"*, Sarvodaya, 20:10 (April1971),   p.447

30. JP, "Different Aspects of a Total Revolution", in JP: TR (SSS), p.87

31. Sebast L. Raj, Total Revolution, Satya Nilayam Prakashan (New Delhi 1980), p.66

32. Ibid.

33. JP, "Towards a New Society", Congress for Cultural Freedom, New Delhi, 1958, p.42

34. Ibid., p.43

35. JP, "Forward", to "Towards Total Revolution- 1: search for an ideology", Popular Prakashan, (Bombay, 1978), p.ix

36. Ibid., p.42

37. JP, "Total Revolution: Some clarifications", in "Towards Total Revolution-iv: Total Revolution, Popular Prakashan, (Bombay, 1978), p.197

38. JP, Prison Diary-1975, p.87 (Oct. 7)

39. JP, "Forward", to "Towards Total Revolution- 1: search for an ideology", Popular Prakashan, (Bombay, 1978), p.200

40. K. Marx, F. Engles & V. Lenin, On Historical Materialism (Moscow, 1972), p.83

41. Vishwanath Tandon, (ed.), Selections from Vinoba (Varanasi, 1981) p.91

42. Suresh Ram, (ed.), Towards Total Revolution (Thanjavuar, 1968)

43. Geoffrey Ostergaard, *Non-Violent Revolution in India* (New Delhi, 1985), p.207

44. Ibid., p.404

45. The Times (London), Oct.13, 1969

46. Nageshwar Prasad, "The Meaning of Total Revolution", Gandhi Marg,1:8(November 1979), p.505

47. K.B.Y. Thottappa, "Epilogue", to Total Revolution, Gandhi Samaj,Madras, 1978, p.85

48. N.G. Goray, "What is Total Revolution (1)", Janata, 30:7(march 16,1975), p.3

49. A. Appadorai, "What He Meant by Total Revolution", The Statesman, (Delhi), Oct.9, 1979

50. V.M. Tarkunde, "Two ways of Revolution",in S. Dasgupte(ed.), Total Revolution symposium, p.108

51. V.B. Karnik, "Total Revolution & Class struggle", in S. Dasgupte (ed.) Total Revolution: A symposium, p.19

52. Prabhu Das Patwari, Some thoughts on Jaya Prakash Narayan, Jaya Prakash Narayan Institute, Madras, 1978, p.7

CONCLUSION

Today our country is facing many problems related to our everyday life. Corruption has become omnipresent. People sitting on government post making illegal wealth through malpractices in their job. Earlier such people were seen as bad and degrading the society and values like honesty and discipline. But now people instead of criticizing and avoiding them, they are now very eager to make friendly relations with them. They wish to be like them. Today, corruption is getting a kind of social acceptance though not openly. It is said by many that "bribery corruption is like oxygen for democracy. If want to have your work done you have to put oil bribe in the machine (government machinery).

Political corruption is the most visible among all of its kinds. Every year we see, increase in the number of 'Baahubalis' (muscle man) reaching in our Parliament and assemblies, through malpractices in elections. It seems completely impossible for a common man having less money to win election in present scenario. After so many decades of independence, we have to think again in which direction we are going? Did our freedom fighters sacrifice their lives for this?

On one hand Indian economy is touching new heights every year; we are joining the power groups in the world on the other hand farmers are committing suicide because of inability to pay their debts. There are places like Gurgaun, Bangalore & Hyderabad, symbol of modern progress but there are places like Kalahandi in Orissa where parent are compelled to sell their child to feed their other children. There is need to stop for a while and think why this happened to our country and what are the responsible factors for it. But the problem today is that nobody has time to think for the underprivileged and the poverty stricken. We are running day & night to gain as much as we can. And we say that life has become very fast. Does fast life mean that we should forget our values; we should forget the poor around us & our social responsibility for them. Growing materialism & a hunger for collecting goods & wealth has contributed very much in the creation of this situation. Market forces are not only shaping our habits of food and clothing but also our traditions and festivals have provided them opportunity to make huge money. On 15th Aug. 1947, when we got freedom, it was hoped that we shape our future according to our own; there were hopes among people that they will get their golden past once again. Poverty eradication and equality for all world targets but today the situation is not satisfactory. Feelings f the people of India got expression in a better form in the speech of Prime Minister Jawahar Lal Nehru which he delivered before the constituent assembly on the night of 14th Aug. 1947, "Longs year ago we made a tryst with destiny, and now the time comes we shall redeem our pledge …. At the stroke of the mid night hour, when the world sleeps, India will awake to life and freedom. A moment comes, which comes but rarely in history, when we step out from the old to the new, when an age ends, and when the sole of a nation, long suppressed, finds utterance. It is fitting that at this solemn moment we take the pledge of dedication to the service of India & her people & to the still larger cause of humanity…. We end today a period of ill fortune and India discovers herself again."[1]

From the early 1970s onwards, wide-spread discontent shook India: large sections of the population came out in demonstrations against rising prices, fall in the supply of essential commodities, unemployment, and more importantly, corruption in government administration. These protests reached a crescendo in two states – Gujarat and Bihar – in 1974, with students leading the agitations and giving them an organized shape. The Gujarat state government ruled by Indira Gandhi's Congress Party was forced to resign that year. In fresh elections to the Gujarat legislature in early June, 1975, the Congress was trounced and the opposition parties formed the new government in that state. Indira realized that she was losing her grip, and was threatened by a political crisis. The threat became imminent when on June 12, 1975, the Allahabad high court of the state of Uttar Pradesh (from where Indira Gandhi won in the parliamentary election in 1971), declared her election invalid on two corruption charges in the conduct of her poll campaign at that time. She was accused of violating the Indian law by first, using an officer of her government to make campaign arrangements, and secondly, by using other state officers to put up speaker's stands in her constituency and supply electricity to her amplifying equipment. The high court judgment debarred her from holding the office of prime minister, but granted a stay of the order for 20 days – to allow her party to choose another leader (since the Congress party still enjoyed a majority in the Indian parliament).

Instead of resigning - as she should have following the court judgment - Indira Gandhi flexed her muscles, preparing for a confrontation with her opponents. The Opposition parties had decided to hold rallies and demonstrations demanding her resignation. In order to preempt them, Indira Gandhi declared an Emergency on June 26 on the ground that `a grave emergency exists whereby the security of India is threatened by internal disturbances'. She did this in accordance with provisions under Part XVIII of the Indian Constitution which allow for the imposition of Emergency and suspension of fundamental rights like freedom of speech. Just before her public announcement declaring Emergency, in a pre-dawn swoop her government arrested hundreds of prominent Opposition politicians and activists, and cut off electricity connection to major newspaper establishments to prevent them from printing their papers carrying the news of the arrests. By the time the connection was resumed and they could bring out their papers, censorship had already been promulgated under the Emergency rules. As a result of this censorship, for almost two years that followed, citizens did not have any knowledge of what was happening beyond their own neighborhoods, families had no information about their members who disappeared (later found out to be arrested and often killed by the security forces), the public were kept in the dark about inhuman acts like forcible sterilization of the poor. The Indira government enacted two laws – one curbing the right of journalists to report proceedings in parliament, and the other imposing restrictions on their reporting anything that might 'bring into hatred or contempt or excite disaffection towards the government' (thus effectively banning all media publicity to anti-government criticism or public protests against government policies). Another draconian law called MISA (Maintenance of Internal Security Act) was used to imprison Opposition leaders and political dissenters.

Censorship prevented Indian journalists from reporting the fact that when parliament met on July 21, the Opposition members voted against the resolution approving Emergency, and walked out.

It was only from the Western media, that the world came to know about the fact that the Opposition strength in parliament at that time was already reduced as a result of the arrest of a large number of their members. In a list of parliamentarians in jail in 14 countries, compiled by Amnesty International on April 6 1976, India had the highest number (59) behind bars. The government deployed censor officers to vet reports and editorials before their publication in newspapers. Those papers which refused to submit to such humiliation were subjected to pressures like disconnection of electricity and withdrawal of government advertisements. Many dissenting journalists were put behind bars.

Under the Emergency rules, workers were denied the right to strike. But the industrialists were given a free hand to dismiss employees. They lay off about 500,000 workers within six months after the declaration of Emergency. Anti-working class ordinances were issued curtailing the workers' minimum bonus from 8.33 per cent of the earnings to 4 per cent. It was not surprising therefore that the Indian industrialists at home, as well as the World Bank abroad, applauded these Emergency measures of the Indira Gandhi government. The large scale Indian private sector industrialists, like the Birla's and the Tata's, welcomed her industrial policies, and the Western-dominated Aid India consortium promised her government an aid of $ 1,600 million – a record of sorts in those days.

These oppressive measures under the Emergency were accompanied by Indira Gandhi's announcement of a `twenty-point programme' – claiming to improve the lot of the poor. Under this programme, she promised to implement land reforms, abolish the practice of bonded labour (under which rural landlord-moneylenders tied poor and landless labourers to eternal bondage if they failed to pay off their debts), fix minimum wages for agricultural labourers, supply clothes to the poor and increase job opportunities for educated young people, among other things. In her speeches, she asserted that it was to be able to implement this pro-poor programme that she had to impose the Emergency, so that the rich who opposed it could be suppressed.

But in reality, how did this economic package work out for the Indian poor? Land reforms and minimum wages remained a distant dream for the rural labourers. The rich village landlords could not be forced to part with the excess land that they held illegally for distribution among the landless, and pay the wages officially fixed for their agricultural labourers – since they were the main pillars of Mrs. Gandhi's Congress party, her prime constituency in rural India. Even those few, who were freed from bonded labour, came out to find that no means were provided to them by the government to enable them to earn a living. They again reverted to the old practice of taking loans from landlords and money-lenders in order to survive – and got entangled in the same bondage being unable to pay off their debts. In the urban areas, rising prices affected the common citizens, and workers often resorted to strikes facing the risk of loss of jobs and imprisonment. The promise of jobs for the unemployed youth also turned out to be false. By October 1975, registered job seekers among the educated had climbed to 4.1 million. Twenty four percent of the urban youth remained unemployed. The twenty-point programme thus cut nowhere near deep enough to solve the manifest problems of the country – whether in the villages or cities.

Public disaffection broke out in demonstrations – mainly in protest against the government's sterilization drive. The police often retaliated against such demonstrations with extreme brutality. In two towns of the northern state of Uttar Pradesh – Muzaffarnagar and Sultanpur - in October 1976, more than seventy people were killed by the police when they came out on the streets resisting forcible sterilization. Although the press was forced to black out such incidents, news reached the people all around – often in the highly exaggerated form of rumors turning popular mood against Mrs. Gandhi and her administration. In the heart of the capital itself, in the Turkman Gate area of Delhi, on April 18, 1976, the police opened fire on protesters who were resisting the demolition of their homes. The demolition drive was launched by Indira Gandhi's son Sanjay Gandhi to cleanse the city of slums and force their poor residents to leave the capital (which was their working place) and move to distant settlements. The residents of Turkman Gate refused to move as they would have to commute every day paying heavy bus fares to reach the capital to earn their living. The Turkman Gate incident – although not reported by the Indian press – was witnessed by the citizens of Delhi who felt repulsed by such developments brought about by the Emergency.

There were several factors that decisively turned the Indian public opinion in the period ending 1976 and beginning 1977, against the emergency regime in general and Indira Gandhi in particular. The first of course was the growing disaffection among the working people- both rural and urban. Then there was the clamp dawn on the media- which alienated the urban middle class readers who had been traditionally brought upon a media fare of pluralistic viewpoints and were now being subjected instead to one sided government press handouts. The next factor was the officially sponsored propaganda eulogizing a dynastic leadership centered on Indira Gandhi and her son sanjay Gandhi. Sanjay Gandhi became a notorious figure in the society for his autocratic style of functioning within the congress party, as well as outside where he led the infamous sterilization drive and demolition of squatters' colonies. Within the congress party, anti- sanjay sentiments were growing leading to disgruntlement among the older leaders.

Meanwhile, pressures were being mounted upon Indira Gandhi by the US and other Western governments to restore democracy. Critics pointed out that the Indian parliamentary elections which were due to be held in March 1976 had been postponed by Indira Gandhi for two years. The Western media and international human rights organizations had been highlighting reports about atrocities on the common people, imprisonment of Opposition leaders and the muffling of press under Indira Gandhi's rule. By the beginning of 1977, the record of her Emergency regime had become a matter of global scandal, and she was losing the stature that she once enjoyed among dignitaries in international gatherings. She had to restore her image in the global community, and legitimize her authority in the domestic scene. The only way out was the holding of elections – which she had been trying to postpone.

In a dramatic gesture, on January 18, 1977, Indira Gandhi announced general elections to be held in mid-March that year under conditions of relaxed Emergency. In making this announcement, she was encouraged by reports provided by the intelligence agencies of her own government which forecast hands-down victory for her Congress party. They assured her that the Opposition was divided and demoralized, with most of their leaders in jail and lacking resources to fight the election. In contrast, her party had all the advantages of political power, control of the mass media, and the immense funds collected from industrial houses and extorted from other sources by her party men during the period under her Emergency regime.

But a self-confident and arrogant Indira Gandhi was in for a surprise, when just a month before the elections, several prominent leaders from her Congress party, headed by the most senior minister in her cabinet, Jagjivan Ram, resigned and joined the Opposition. This sealed her fate. The resignations boosted the morale of the Opposition and encouraged the common people to shed fear and speak their minds. During the poll campaign, the hitherto-suppressed news of police brutality, forcible sterilization and bulldozing of slums came out in public gaze. With this exposure, the majority of the electorate turned decidedly against Indira Gandhi's Congress. In the 1977 March parliamentary election, of an electorate of 320 million, roughly 60 percent voted Indira Gandhi's Congress out of power. She herself, along with her son Sanjay and other important ministers, suffered defeat at the polls. The 1977 election brought for the first time a non-Congress government in New Delhi. Ever since its independence in August 1947, it had been ruled by the Congress, first led by Jawaharlal Nehru, and then by his daughter Indira (barring a brief interlude after Nehru's death in 1964 when his devotee Lal Bahadur Shastri became the prime minister for a while).

Though Emergency is remembered in India as the darkest era of postcolonial Indian history but it is equally true that it was only the people of this land who declared their faith in democratic and liberal traditions by overthrowing the autocratic regime of Indira Gandhi. Perhaps someday politicians of India will realize and accept this fact that ultimate key to our democracy is in the hands of public and Emergency is a reminder for those autocratic tendencies who try to strengthen themselves. In a democratic setup if aspirations of masses are not addressed then masses won't hesitate in using the weapon of voting to overthrow the dictatorial regimes.

BIBLIOGRAPHY

BOOKS

S.K. Ghosh, "The Crusade and the End of Indira Raj", (New Delhi: Intellectual Book Centre, 1978)

Granville Austin, The Indian Experience, (OUP, 2000)

Morarji Desai to Oriana Fallaci, New Republic quoted in Francine R. Frankel, India's Political Economy 1947-1977, Delhi, 1978

Bipan Chandra, et.al. (ed.), India After Independence1947-2000, (New Delhi: Penguin Books,2000)

J.A. Naik (An alternative Polity for India, S.chand & Company Ltd. March 1976

Ajit Bhattacharjea, Jay Prakash Narayan; A Political Biography,Vikas publishing house Pvt.Ltd.,1975

Bimal Prasad, (ed.), A Revolutionary's Quest: Selected Writings Of Jaya Prakash Narayan(New Delhi, 1980)

Bimal Prasad, et.al.(ed.) Jaya Prakash Narayan Essential writings (1929-1979) A Centenary Volume (1902-2002) Konark Publishers PVT LTD, Delhi, 2002

Francine R. Frankel, India's Political Economy 1947-1977, Delhi, 1978

Mary.C.Carras, Indira Gandhi –in the Crucible of Leadership, Bombay,1980

Tariq Ali, The Nehrus and the Gandhis-An Indian Dynasty, London,1985,

Jaya Prakash Narayan,Prison Diary(Bombay,1977)

S.K.Ghosh, The crusade and the End of Indira Raj,(New Delhi :Intellectual book Centre,1978)

J.D.Sethi, Gandhi Today,Vikas Publising house,New Delhi,1978

JP, "Towards Total Revolution-1: Search for an Ideology", Popular Prakashan,Bombay,1978

NEWSPAPERS

1. The Hindu
2. The Times Of India
3. Indian Express

MAGAZINES/JOURNALS

1. India Today
2. Outlook
3. Samved, November 2004
4. Politics India(Monthly Journal)

PHOTOS

Photographs taken from Google Images.

ABOUT AUTHOR

Kranti Deep Verma has done Masters in Public Administration (M.P.A.) from University of Lucknow, Lucknow and Master of Arts (M.A.) in History from Jamia Millia Islamia, New Delhi. He has done M.Phil. in History from Alagappa University, Tamil Nadu. His areas of interest are social and political movements of modern India, Gender issues & human rights issues. He has written articles in many national magazines and contributed chapters in edited books. Currently he is teaching as Assistant Professor in the Department of History, Bhim Rao Ambedkar College, University of Delhi, Delhi.

Email: krantideep@gmail.com

www.ingramcontent.com/pod-product-compliance
Lightning Source LLC
Chambersburg PA
CBHW060748050426
42449CB00008B/1323